Henry Lee

Sea Fables Explained

Henry Lee

Sea Fables Explained

ISBN/EAN: 9783744792547

Printed in Europe, USA, Canada, Australia, Japan

Cover: Foto ©Andreas Hilbeck / pixelio.de

More available books at **www.hansebooks.com**

A MERMAID.
From a Picture by Otto Sinding.

International Fisheries Exhibition

LONDON, 1883

SEA FABLES EXPLAINED

BY

HENRY LEE, F.L.S., F.G.S., F.Z.S.

SOMETIME NATURALIST OF THE BRIGHTON AQUARIUM

AND

AUTHOR OF 'THE OCTOPUS, OR THE DEVIL-FISH OF FICTION AND FACT;'
'SEA MONSTERS UNMASKED,' ETC.

ILLUSTRATED

LONDON
WILLIAM CLOWES AND SONS, Limited
INTERNATIONAL FISHERIES EXHIBITION
AND 13 CHARING CROSS, S.W.
1883

LONDON:
PRINTED BY WILLIAM CLOWES AND SONS, Limited,
STAMFORD STREET AND CHARING CROSS.

PREFACE.

THE little book 'Sea Monsters Unmasked,' recently issued as one of the Handbooks in connection with the Great International Fisheries Exhibition has met with so favourable a reception, that I have been honoured by the request to continue the subject, and to treat also of some of the Fables of the Sea, which once were universally believed, and even now are not utterly extinct.

The topic is not here exhausted. Other sea fables and fallacies might be mentioned and explained; but the amount of letter-press, and the number of illustrations that can be printed without loss for the small sum of one shilling—the price at which these Handbooks are uniformly published—is necessarily limited. I have, therefore, thought it better to endeavour to make each chapter as complete as possible than to crowd into the space allotted to me a greater variety of subjects less fully and carefully discussed.

I have the pleasure of acknowledging the kind assistance I have again received in the matter of illustrations. I gratefully appreciate Mr. Murray's permission to use the woodcut of Hercules slaying the Hydra, taken from Smith's 'Classical Dictionary,' and those of the golden ornaments found by Dr. Schliemann at Mycenæ, and figured in the very interesting book in which his excavations there are described. I have also to thank the proprietors of the *Illustrated London News*, the *Leisure Hour*, and *Land and Water*, for the use of illustrations especially mentioned in the text.

HENRY LEE.

SAVAGE CLUB;
Sept. 4th, 1883.

CONTENTS.

	PAGE
THE MERMAID	1
THE LERNEAN HYDRA	48
SCYLLA AND CHARYBDIS	59
THE "SPOUTING" OF WHALES	62
THE "SAILING" OF THE NAUTILUS	76
BARNACLE GEESE—GOOSE BARNACLES	98

LIST OF ILLUSTRATIONS.

FIG.		PAGE
	A Mermaid. *From a picture by Otto Sinding*	Frontispiece
1.	Noah, His Wife and Three Sons, as Fish-tailed Deities. *From a gem in the Florentine Gallery. After Calmet*	2
2.	Hea, or Noah, the God of the Flood. *Khorsabad*	3
3.	Dagon. *From a bas-relief. Nimroud*	4
4.	Dagon: Half Man, Half Fish. *From Lamy's 'Apparatus Biblicus'*	5
5.	Dagon. *From an agate signet. Nineveh*	,,
6.	Fish Avatar of Vishnu. *After Calmet and Maurice*	6
7.	Atergatis, The Goddess of the Syrians. *From a Phœnician Coin*	8
8.	Venus Rising from the Sea, Supported by Tritons. *After Calmet*	9
9.	Venus Drawn in Her Chariot by Tritons. *From two Corinthian Coins*	10
10.	Ditto.	11
11.	Seal, Drawn as a Fish. *From the Catacombs at Rome*	,,
12.	Mermaid and Fishes of Amboyna. *After Valentyn*	17
13.	A Japanese Artificial Mermaid	27
14.	An Artificial Mermaid. *Probably Japanese*	28
15.	Portrait of a Mermaid said to have been Captured in Japan	29
16.	The Dugong. *From Sir J. Emerson Tennent's 'Ceylon'*	43
17.	The Manatee	45
18.	Figure of a Calamary, From the Temple of Bayr-el-Bahree	50
19.	Figure of an Octopus on a Gold Ornament found by Dr. Schliemann at Mycenæ	51
20.	Ditto.	52
21.	Ditto.	53
22.	Ditto.	,,
23.	Hercules Slaying the Lernean Hydra	57

b

		PAGE
24. THE PHYSETER INUNDATING A SHIP. *After Olaus Magnus*	.	64
25. A WHALE POURING WATER INTO A SHIP FROM ITS BLOW-HOLE. *After Olaus Magnus*	.	64
26. SPERM WHALES "SPOUTING".	.	65
27. THE PAPER NAUTILUS (*Argonauta argo*) SAILING	.	76
28. DITTO. RETRACTED WITHIN ITS SHELL.	.	81
29. DITTO. CRAWLING.	.	86
30. DITTO. SWIMMING.	.	87
31. SHELL OF THE PAPER NAUTILUS (*Argonauta argo*)	.	88
32. SHELL OF THE PEARLY NAUTILUS (*Nautilus pompilius*)	.	89
33. THE PEARLY NAUTILUS (*Nautilus pompilius*) AND SECTION OF ITS SHELL	.	90
34. THE GOOSE-TREE. *From Gerard's 'Herball'*	.	104
35. DITTO. *Fac-simile from Aldrovandus*.	.	110
36. DEVELOPMENT OF BARNACLES INTO GEESE. *Fac-simile from Aldrovandus*	.	111
37. SECTION OF A SESSILE BARNACLE. *Balanus tintinnabulum*	.	113
38. PEDUNCULATED BARNACLE. *Lepas anatifera*	.	115
39. A SHIP'S FIGURE-HEAD PARTLY COVERED WITH BARNACLES.		116
40. WHALE BARNACLE. *Coronula diadema*	.	117
41. A YOUNG BARNACLE. *Larva of Chthamalus stellatus*.	.	118

SEA FABLES EXPLAINED.

THE MERMAID.

NEXT to the pleasure which the earnest zoologist derives from study of the habits and structure of living animals, and his intelligent appreciation of their perfect adaptation to their modes of life, and the circumstances in which they are placed, is the interest he feels in eliminating fiction from truth, whilst comparing the fancies of the past with the facts of the present. As his knowledge increases, he learns that the descriptions by ancient writers of so-called "fabulous creatures" are rather distorted portraits than invented falsehoods, and that there is hardly one of the monsters of old which has not its prototype in Nature at the present day. The idea of the Lernean Hydra, whose heads grew again when cut off by Hercules, originated, as I have shown in another chapter, in a knowledge of the octopus; and in the form and movements of other animals with which we are now familiar we may, in like manner, recognise the similitude and archetype of the mermaid.

But we must search deeply into the history of mankind to discover the real source of a belief that has prevailed in almost all ages, and in all parts of the world, in the existence of a race of beings uniting the form of man with that of the fish. A rude resemblance between these creatures of imagination and tradition and certain aquatic animals is not sufficient to account for that belief. It probably had its origin in ancient mythologies, and in the sculptures and pictures connected with them, which were designed to represent certain attributes of the deities of various nations. In the course of time the meaning of these was lost; and subsequent generations regarded as

FIG. I.—NOAH, HIS WIFE, AND THREE SONS, AS FISH-TAILED DEITIES. *From a Gem in the Florentine Gallery. After Calmet.*

the portraits of existing beings effigies which were at first intended to be merely emblematic and symbolical.

Early idolatry consisted, first, in separating the idea of the One Divinity into that of his various attributes, and of inventing symbols and making images of each separately; secondly, in the worship of the sun, moon, stars, and planets, as living existences; thirdly, in the deification of ancestors and early kings; and these three forms were often mingled together in strange and tangled confusion.

Amongst the famous personages with whose history men were made acquainted by oral tradition was Noah. He was known as the second father of the human race, and the preserver and teacher of the arts and sciences as they existed before the Great Deluge, of which so many separate traditions exist among the various races of mankind. Consequently, he was an object of worship in many countries and under many names; and his wife and sons, as his assistants in the diffusion of knowledge, were sometimes associated with him.

According to Berosus, of Babylon,—the Chaldean priest and astronomer, who extracted from the sacred books of "that great city" much interesting ancient lore, which he introduced into his 'History of Syria,' written, about B.C. 260, for the use of the Greeks,—at a time when men were sunk in barbarism, there came up from the Erythrean Sea (the Persian Gulf), and landed on the Babylonian shore, a creature named Oannes, which had the body and head of a fish. But above the fish's head was the head of a man, and below the tail of the fish were human feet. It had also human arms, a human voice, and human language. This strange monster sojourned among the rude people during the day, taking no food, but retiring to the sea at night; and it continued for some time thus to visit them, teaching them the arts of civilized life, and instructing them in science and religion.*

FIG. 2.—HEA, OR NOAH, THE GOD OF THE FLOOD. *Khorsabad.*

In this tale we have a distorted account of the life and occupation of Noah after his escape from the deluge which destroyed his home and drowned his neighbours. Oannes was one of the names under which

* Berosus, lib. i. p. 48.

he was worshipped in Chaldea, at Erech ("the place of the ark"), as the sacred and intelligent fish-god, the teacher of mankind, the god of science and knowledge. There he was also called Oes, Hoa, Ea, Ana, Anu, Aun, and Oan. Noah was worshipped, also, in Syria and Mesopotamia, and in Egypt, at "populous No," * or Thebes—so named from "Theba," "the ark."

FIG. 3.—DAGON. *From a bas relief, Nimroud.*

The history of the coffin of Osiris is another version of Noah's ark, and the period during which that Egyptian divinity is said to have been shut up in it, after it was set afloat upon the waters, was precisely the same as that during which Noah remained in the ark.

Dagon, also — sometimes called Odacon—the great fish-god of the Philistines and Babylonians, was another phase of Oannes. "Dag," in Hebrew, signifies "a male fish," and "Aun" and "Oan" were two of the names of Noah. "Dag-aun" or "Dag-oan" therefore means "the fish Noah." He was portrayed in two ways. The more ancient image of him was that of a man issuing from a fish, as described of Oannes by Berosus; but in later times it was varied to that of a man whose upper half was human, and the lower parts those of

* Nahum iii. 8.

a fish. The image of Dagon which fell upon its face to the ground before "the ark of the God of Israel," was probably of this latter form, for we read * that in its fall, "the head of Dagon and both the palms of his hands were cut off upon the threshold: only the *stump* (in the margin, "*the fishy part*") of Dagon was left to him. This was evidently Milton's conception of him:

"Dagon his name; sea-monster, upward man
And downward fish." †

FIG. 4.—DAGON. *After Calmet.*

In some of the Nineveh sculptures of the fish-god, the head of the fish forms a kind of mitre on the head of the man, whilst the body of the fish appears as a cloak or cape over his shoulders and

FIG. 5.—DAGON. *From an Agate Signet, Nineveh.*

back. The fish varies in length; in some cases the tail almost touches the ground; in others it reaches but little below the man's waist.

* 1 Samuel v. 4.
† 'Paradise Lost,' Book i. l. 462.

FIG. 6.—FISH AVATAR OF VISHNU.
After Calmet and Maurice.

In one of his "avatars," or incarnations, the god Vishnu "the Preserver," is represented as issuing from the mouth of a fish. He is celebrated as having miraculously preserved one righteous family, and, also, the Vedas, the sacred records, when the world was drowned. Not only is this legend of the Indian god wrought up with the history of Noah, but Vishnu and Noah bear the same name — Vishnu being the Sanscrit form of "Ish-nuh," "the man Noah." The word "avatar" also means "out of the boat." In fact the whole mythology of Greece and Rome, as well as of Asia, is full of the history and deeds of Noah, which it is impossible to misunderstand. In all the representations of a deity having a combined human and piscine form, the original idea was that of a person coming out of a fish—not being part of one, but issuing from it, as Noah issued from the ark. In all of them the fish denoted "preservation," "fecundity," "plenty," and "diffusion of knowledge."* As the image was not the effigy of a divine personage, but symbolized certain attributes of Divinity, its sex was comparatively unimportant, although it is possible that, combined with the fecundity of the fish, the idea of Noah's wife, as the second mother of all subsequent generations, according to the widely-spread and accepted traditions of the deluge, may have influenced the impersonation.

Atergatis, the far-famed goddess of the Syrians, was also a fish-divinity. Her image, like that of Dagon, had at first a fish's body with human extremities protruding from it; but in the course of centuries it was gradually altered to that of a being the upper portion of whose body was that of a woman and the lower half that of a fish. Gatis was a powerful queen of Sidon, and mother of Semiramis. She received the title of "Ater," or "Ader," "the Great," for the benefits she conferred on her people; one of these benefits being a strict conservation of their fisheries, both from their own imprudent use, and from foreign interference. She issued an edict that no fish should be eaten without her consent, and that no one should take fish in the neighbouring sea without a licence from herself. It is not improbable that she and her celebrated daughter, who

* Some writers are of the opinion that the legend of Oannes contains an allusion to the rising and setting of the sun, and that his semi-piscine form was the expression of the idea that half his time was spent above ground, and half below the waves. The same commentators also regard all the "civilizing" gods and goddesses as, respectively, solar and lunar deities. The attributes symbolized in the worship of Noah and the sun are so nearly alike that the two interpretations are not incompatible.

is said by Ovid and others to have been the builder of the walls of Babylon, were worshipped together; for that Atergatis was the same as the fish-goddess Ashteroth, or Ashtoreth, "the builder of the encompassing wall," we have, amongst other proofs, a remarkable one in Biblical history. In the first book of Maccabees v. 43, 44, we read that "all the heathen being discomfited before him (Judas Maccabeus) cast away their weapons, and fled unto the temple that was at *Carnaim*. But they took the city, and burned the temple with all that were therein. Thus was *Carnaim* subdued, neither could they stand any longer before Judas." In the second book of Maccabees xii. 26, we are told that "Maccabeus marched forth to *Carnion*, and to the temple of *Atargatis*, and there he slew five and twenty thousand persons." In Genesis xiv. 5, this city and temple are referred to as "*Ashteroth Karnaim*."

FIG. 7.—ATERGATIS.
From a Phœnician coin.

Fig. 7 is a representation of Atergatis on a medal coined at Marseilles. It shows that when the Phœnician colony from Syria, by whom that city was founded, settled there, they brought with them the worship of the gods of their country.

Atergatis was worshipped by the Greeks as Derceto and Astarte. Lucian writes*:—"In Phœnicia I saw the image of Derceto, a strange sight, truly! For she had the half of a woman, and from the thighs downwards a fish's tail." Diodorus Siculus describes (lib. ii.) the same deity, as represented at Ascalon, as "having the face of a woman,

---

* 'Opera Omnia,' tom. ii. p. 884, edit. Bened. de Deá Syr.

but all the rest of the body a fish's." And this very same image at Ascalon, which Diodorus calls Derceto, or Atergatis, is denominated by Herodotus[*] "the celestial Aphrodite," who was identical with the Cyprian and Roman Venus. Of all the sacred buildings erected to the goddess, this temple was by far the most ancient; and the Cyprians

FIG. 8.—VENUS RISING FROM THE SEA, SUPPORTED BY TRITONS.
After Calmet.

themselves acknowledged that their temple was built after the model of it by certain Phœnicians who came from that part of Syria.

Thus the worship of Noah, as the second father of mankind, the repopulator of the earth, passed through various

[*] Lib. i. cap. cv.

phases and transformations till it merged in that of Venus, who rose from the sea, and was regarded as the representative of the reproductive power of Nature—the goddess whom Lucretius thus addressed :

> "Blest Venus! Thou the sea and fruitful earth
> Peoplest amain; to thee whatever lives
> Its being owes, and that it sees the sun :"

and to whom refers the passage in the Orphic hymn :

> "From thee are all things—all things thou producest
> Which are in heaven, or in the fertile earth,
> Or in the sea, or in the great abyss."

Under this latter phase—the impersonation of Venus—the fish portion of the body was discarded, and the cast-off form was allotted in popular credence to the Tritons—minor deities, who acknowledged the supremacy of the goddess, and were ready to render her homage and service by bearing her in their arms, drawing her chariot, etc., but who still possessed considerable power as sea-gods, and could calm the waves and rule the storm, at pleasure.

VENUS DRAWN IN HER CHARIOT BY TRITONS. *From two Corinthian coins.*

Figs. 9 and 10 are from two Corinthian medals, each shewing Venus in a car or chariot drawn by Tritons, one male, the other female. On the obverse of Fig. 9, is the head of Nero, and on that of Fig. 10, the head of his grandmother Agrippina.*

From the very earliest period of history, then, the conjoined human and fish form was known to every generation of men. It was presented to their sight in childhood by sculptures and pictures, and was a conspicuous object in their religious worship. By the lapse of time its original import was lost and debased; and, from being

* It is worthy of note that the fish was also adopted as an emblem by the early Christians, and was frequently sculptured on their tombs as a private mark or sign of the faith in which the person there interred had died. It alluded to the letters which composed the Greek word Ιχθυς ("a fish") forming an anagram, the initials of words which conveyed the following sentiment: Ιησους, Jesus; Χριστος, Christ; Θεου, of God; Υιος, Son; Σωτηρ, Saviour. But it doubtless bore, also, the older meaning of "preservation" and "reproduction," of which the fish was the symbol, and betokened a belief in a future resurrection, as Noah was preserved to dwell in, and populate, a new world. In 'Sea Monsters Unmasked,' page 55, I gave a figure, copied by permission from the *Illustrated London News*, of a rough sculpture in the Roman catacombs, of Jonah being disgorged by a sea-monster. Near to it was found, on another Christian tomb, one of these designs of the "fish;" and it is not a little curious that, whereas the animal depicted as casting forth Jonah is not a whale, but a sea-serpent, or dragon, the *ichtheus* in this instance is apparently not a fish, but a seal.

FIG. 11.—CHRISTIAN SYMBOL. *From the Catacombs at Rome.*

The article referred to appeared in the *Illustrated London News* of February 3rd, 1872, and the woodcut (fig. 11), an electrotype of which was most kindly presented to me by the proprietors of that paper, was one of the sketches that accompanied it.

an emblem and symbol, it came to be accepted as the corporeal shape and structure of actually-existent sea-deities, who might present themselves to the view of the mariner, in visible and tangible form, at any moment. Thus were men trained and prepared to believe in mermen and mermaids, to expect to meet with them at sea, and to recognise as one of them any animal the appearance and movements of which could possibly be brought into conformity with their pre-conceived ideas.

Accordingly, and very naturally, we find that from north to south this belief has been entertained. Megasthenes, who was a contemporary of Aristotle, but his junior, and whose geographical work was probably written at about the period of the great philosopher's death, reported that the sea which surrounded Taprobana, the ancient Ceylon, was inhabited by creatures having the appearance of women. Ælian stated that there were "whales," or "great fishes," having the form of satyrs. The early Portuguese settlers in India asserted that true mermen were found in the Eastern seas, and old Norse legends tell of submarine beings of conjoined human and piscine form, who dwell in a wide territory far below the region of the fishes, over which the sea, like the cloudy canopy of our sky, loftily rolls, and some of whom have, from time to time, landed on Scandinavian shores, exchanged their fishy extremities for human limbs, and acquired amphibious habits. Not only have poets sung of the wondrous and seductive beauty of the maidens of these aquatic tribes, but many a Jack tar has come home from sea prepared to affirm on oath that he has seen a mermaid. To the best of his belief he has told the truth. He has seen some living being which looked wonderfully human, and his imagination, aided by an inherited superstition, has supplied the rest.

Before endeavouring to identify the object of his delusion, it may be well to mention a few instances of the supposed appearance of mermen and mermaidens in various localities. Pliny writes *: "When Tiberius was emperor, an embassy was sent to him from Olysippo (Lisbon) expressly to inform him that a Triton, which was recognised as such by its form, had shown itself in a certain cave, and had been heard to produce loud sounds on a conch-shell. The Nereid, also, is not imaginary: its body is rough and covered with scales, but it has the appearance of a human being. For one was seen upon the same coast; and when it was dying those dwelling near at hand heard it moaning sadly for a long time. And the Governor of Gaul wrote to the divine Augustus that several Nereids had been found dead upon the shore. I have many informants—illustrious persons in high positions—who have assured me that they saw in the Sea of Cadiz a merman whose whole body was exactly like that of a man, that these mermen mount on board ships by night, and weigh down that end of the vessel on which they rest, and that if they are allowed to remain there long they will sink the ship."

Ælian in one of his short, jerky, disconnected chapters,† which rarely exceed a page in length, and some of which only contain two lines, writes : " It is reported that the great sea which surrounds the island of Taprobana (Ceylon) contains an immense multitude of fishes and whales, and some of them have the heads of lions, panthers, rams, and other animals; and (which is more wonderful still) some of the cetaceans have the form of satyrs. There are others which have the face of a woman, but prickles instead of hair. In addition to these, it is said there are other

* *Naturalis Historia*, Lib. ix. cap. v.
† *De Naturâ Animalium*, Lib. xvi. cap. xviii.

creatures of so strange and monstrous a kind that it would be impossible exactly to explain their appearance without the aid of a skilfully drawn picture: these have elongated and coiled tails, and, for feet, have claws * or fins. And I hear that in the same sea there are great amphibious beasts which are gregarious, and live on grain, and by night feed on the corn crops and grass, and are also very fond of the ripe fruit of the palms. To obtain these they encircle in their embrace the trees which are young and flexible, and, shaking them violently, enjoy the fruit which they thus cause to fall. When morning dawns they return to the sea, and plunge beneath the waves."

Ælian seems to have derived this information from Megasthenes, already referred to; but in another chapter,† he writes with greater certainty concerning these semi-human whales, and claims divine authority for his belief in the existence of tritons. "Although," he says, "we have no rational explanation nor absolute proof of that which fishermen are said to be able to affirm concerning the form of the tritons, we have the sworn testimony of many persons that there are in the sea cetaceans which from the head down to the middle of the body resemble the human species. Demostratus, in his works on fishing, says that an aged triton was seen near the town of Tanagra, in Bœotia, which was like the drawings and pictures of tritons, but its features were so obscured by age, and it disappeared so quickly, that its true character was not easily perceptible. But on the spot where it had rested on the shore were found some rough and very hard scales which had become detached from it. A certain senator—one of those selected by lot to carry on

---

* "*Forfices*," literally "shears," or "nippers," like the claws of a lobster.

† Lib. xiii. cap. xxi.

the administration of Achaia and the duties of the annual magistracy" (the mayor, in fact,) "being anxious to investigate the nature of this triton, put a portion of its skin on the fire. It gave out a most horrible odour; and those standing by were unable to decide whether it belonged to a terrestrial or marine animal. But the magistrate's curiosity had an evil ending, for very soon afterwards, whilst crossing a narrow creek in a boat, he fell overboard and was drowned; and the Tanagreans all regarded this as a judgment upon him for his crime of impiety towards the triton—an interpretation which was confirmed when his decomposing body was cast ashore, for it emitted exactly the same odour as had the burned skin of the triton. The Tanagreans and Demostratus explain whence the triton had strayed, and how it was stranded in this place. I believe," continues Ælian, "that tritons exist, and I reverentially produce as my witness a most veracious god—namely, Apollo Didymæus, whom no man in his senses would presume to regard as unworthy of credit. He sings thus of the triton, which he calls the sheep of the sea:

'*Dum vocale maris monstrum natat æquore triton,
Neptuni pecus, in funes forte incidit extra
Demissos navim*';"

which I venture to translate as follows:

A triton, vocal monster of the deep,
One of a flock of Neptune's scaly sheep,
Was caught, whilst swimming o'er the watery plain,
By lines which fishers from their boat had lain.

"Therefore," Ælian concludes, "if he, the omniscient god, pronounces that there are tritons, it does not behove us to doubt their existence."

Sir J. Emerson Tennent, in his 'Natural History of Ceylon,' quoting from the *Histoire de la Compagnie de*

Jésus, mentions that the annalist of the exploits of the Jesuits in India gravely records that seven of these monsters, male and female, were captured at Manaar, in 1560, and carried to Goa, where they were dissected by Demas Bosquez, physician to the Viceroy, "and their internal structure found to be in all respects conformable to the human." He also quotes Valentyn, one of the Dutch colonial chaplains, who, in his account of the Natural History of Amboyna,* embodied in his great work on the Netherlands' possessions in India, published in 1727,† devoted the first section of his chapter on the fishes of that island to a minute description of the "Zee-Menschen," "Zee-Wyven," and mermaids, the existence of which he warmly insists on as being beyond cavil. He relates that in 1663, when a lieutenant in the Dutch service was leading a party of soldiers along the sea-shore in Amboyna, he and all his company saw the mermen swimming at a short distance from the beach. They had long and flowing hair of a colour between grey and green. Six weeks afterwards the creatures were again seen by him and more than fifty witnesses, at the same place, by clear daylight. "If any narrative in the world," adds Valentyn, "deserves credit it is this; since not only one, but two mermen together were seen by so many eye-witnesses. Should the stubborn world, however, hesitate to believe it, it matters nothing, as there are people who would even deny that such cities as Rome, Constantinople, or Cairo, exist, merely because they themselves have not happened to see them. But what are such incredulous persons," he continues, "to make

---

* One of the Dutch spice-islands in the Banda Sea, between Celebes and Papua.

† *Beschrijving van Oud en Nieuw Oost-Indien*, etc., 5 vols. folio, Dordrecht and Amsterdam, 1727, vol. iii. p. 330.

of the circumstance recorded by Albrecht Herport * in his account of India, that a merman was seen in the water near the church of Taquan on the morning of the 29th of April, 1661, and a mermaid at the same spot the same afternoon? Or what do they say to the fact that in 1714 a mermaid was not only seen but captured near the island of Booro, five feet, Rhineland measure, in height; which lived four days and seven hours, but, refusing all food, died without leaving any intelligible account of herself?"

FIG. 12.—MERMAID AND FISHES OF AMBOYNA. *After Valentyn.*

Valentyn, in support of his own faith in the mermaid, cites many other instances in which both "sea-men and sea-women" were seen and taken at Amboyna; especially one by a district visitor of the church, who presented it to the Governor Vanderstel. Of this "well-authenticated" specimen he gives an elaborate portrait amongst the fishes of the island,†

* *Itinerarium Indicum,* Berne, 1669.
† With the permission and assistance of Messrs. Longman, the accompanying wood-cut of this picture, and that of the Dugong, on page 43, are copied from Sir J. Emerson Tennent's book published in 1861.

with a minute description of each for the satisfaction of men of science.

The fame of this creature having reached Europe, the British minister in Holland wrote to Valentyn on the 28th of December, 1716, whilst the Emperor Peter the Great, of Russia, was his guest at Amsterdam, to communicate the desire of the Czar that the mermaid should be brought home from Amboyna for his inspection. To complete his proofs of the existence of mermen and merwomen, Valentyn points triumphantly to the historical fact that in Holland, in the year 1404, a mermaid was driven, during a tempest, through a breach in the dyke of Edam, and was taken alive in the lake of Purmer. Thence she was carried to Haarlem, where the Dutch women taught her to spin, and where several years after, she died in the Roman Catholic faith;— "but this," says the pious Calvinistic chaplain, "in no way militates against the truth of her story." The worthy minister citing the authority of various writers as proof that mermaids had in all ages been known in Gaul, Naples, Epirus, and the Morea, comes to the conclusion that as there are "sea-cows," "sea-horses," "sea-dogs," as well as "sea-trees," and "sea-flowers," which he himself had seen, there are no reasonable grounds for doubt that there may also be "sea-maidens" and "sea-men."

In an early account of Newfoundland,* Whitbourne describes a "maremaid or mareman," which he had seen "within the length of a pike," and which "came swimming swiftly towards him, looking cheerfully on his face, as it had been a woman. By the face, eyes, nose, mouth, chin, ears, neck and forehead, it appeared to be so beautiful, and in those parts so well proportioned, having round about the head many blue streaks resembling hair, but certainly it

* Whitbourne's 'Discourse of Newfoundland.'

was no hair. The shoulders and back down to the middle were square, white, and smooth as the back of a man, and from the middle to the end it tapered like a broad-hooked arrow." The animal put both its paws on the side of the boat wherein its observer sat, and strove much to get in, but was repelled by a blow.

In 1676, a description was given by an English surgeon named Glover, of an animal of this kind. The author did not designate it by any name, but the incident has the honour of being recorded in the *Philosophical Transactions*.* About three leagues from the mouth of the river Rappahannock, in America, while alone in a vessel, he observed, at the distance of about half a stone-throw, he says, "a most prodigious creature, much resembling a man, only somewhat larger, standing right up in the water, with his head, neck, shoulders, breast and waist, to the cubits of his arms, above water, and his skin was tawny, much like that of an Indian; the figure of his head was pyramidal and sleek, without hair; his eyes large and black, and so were his eyebrows; his mouth very wide, with a broad black streak on the upper lip, which turned upwards at each end like mustachios. His countenance was grim and terrible. His neck, shoulders, arms, breast and waist, were like unto the neck, arms, shoulders, breast and waist of a man. His hands, if he had any, were under water. He seemed to stand with his eyes fixed on me for some time, and afterwards dived down, and, a little after, rose at somewhat a greater distance, and turned his head towards me again, and then immediately fell a little under water, that I could discern him throw out his arms and gather them in as a man does when he swims. At last, he shot with his head downwards, by which means he cast his tail above the

* Glover's 'Account of Virginia,' ap. Phil. Trans. vol. xi. p. 625.

water, which exactly resembled the tail of a fish, with a broad fane at the end of it."

Thormodus Torfæus * maintains that mermaids are found on the south coast of Iceland, and, according to Olafsen,† two have been taken in the surrounding seas, the first in the earlier part of the history of that island, and the second in 1733. The latter was found in the stomach of a shark. Its lower parts were consumed, but the upper were entire. They were as large as those of a boy eight or nine years old. Both the cutting teeth and grinders were long and shaped like pins, and the fingers were connected by a large web. Olafsen was inclined to believe that these were human remains, but the islanders all firmly maintained that they were part of " a marmennill," by which name the mermaid is known among them.

Of course the worthy bishop of Bergen, Pontoppidan, has something to tell us about mermaids in his part of the world. "Amongst the sea monsters," he says, ‡ "which are in the North Sea, and are often seen, I shall give the first place to the Hav-manden, or merman, whose mate is called Hav-fruen, or mermaid. The existence of this creature is questioned by many, nor is it at all to be wondered at, because most of the accounts we have had of it are mixed with mere fables, and may be looked upon as idle tales." As such he regards the story told by Jonas Ramus in his 'History of Norway,' of a mermaid taken by fishermen at Hordeland, near Bergen, and which is said to have sung an unmusical song to King Hiorlief. In the same category he places an account given by Besenius in his life of Frederic II. (1577), of a mermaid that called

---

* *Historia rerum Norvegicarum.*

† *Voyage en Islande*, tom. iii. p. 223.

‡ 'Natural History of Norway,' vol. ii. p. 190.

herself Isbrandt, and held several conversations with a peasant at Samsoe, in which she foretold the birth of King Christian IV., "and made the peasant preach repentance to the courtiers, who were very much given to drunkenness." Equally "idle" with the above stories is, in his opinion, another, extracted from an old manuscript still to be seen in the University Library at Copenhagen, and quoted by Andrew Bussæus (1619), of a merman caught by the two senators, Ulf Rosensparre and Christian Holch, whilst on their voyage home to Denmark from Norway. This sea-man frightened the two worshipful gentlemen so terribly that they were glad to let him go again; for as he lay upon the deck he spoke Danish to them, and threatened that if they did not give him his liberty "the ship should be cast away, and every soul of the crew should perish."

"When such fictions as these," says Pontoppidan, "are mixed with the history of the merman, and when that creature is represented as a prophet and an orator; when they give the mermaid a melodious voice, and tell us that she is a fine singer, we need not wonder that so few people of sense will give credit to such absurdities, or that they even doubt the existence of such a creature." The good prelate, however, goes on to say that "whilst we have no ground to believe all these fables, yet, as to the existence of the creature we may safely give our assent to it," and, "if this be called in question, it must proceed entirely from the fabulous stories usually mixed with the truth." Like Valentyn, he argues that as there are "sea-horses," "sea-cows," "sea-wolves," "sea-dogs," "sea-hogs," etc., it is probable from analogy, that "we should find in the ocean a fish or creature which resembles the human species more than any other." As for the objection "founded on self-love and respect to our own species which is honoured with the image of God, who made man lord of all creatures, and that, consequently, we may suppose he is entitled to a noble and heavenly form which other creatures must not partake of," he thinks "its force vanishes when we consider the form of apes, and especially of another African creature called 'Quoyas Morrov' described by Odoard Dapper" in his work on Africa, and which appears to have been a chimpanzee. Pontoppidan regarded it as being the Satyr of the ancients. He therefore claims that "if we will not allow our Norwegian Hastromber the honourable name of merman, we may very well call it the 'Sea-ape,' or the 'Sea-Quoyas-Morrov;' especially as the author already quoted says that, "in the Sea of Angola mermaids are frequently caught which resemble the human species. They are taken in nets, and killed by the negroes, and are heard to shriek and cry like women."

The Bishop adds that in the diocese of Bergen, as well as in the manor of Nordland, there were hundreds of persons who affirmed with the strongest assurances that they had seen this kind of creature; sometimes at a distance and at other times quite close to their boats, standing upright, and formed like a human creature down to the middle—the rest they could not see—but of those who had seen them out of water and handled them he had not been able to find more than one person of credit who could vouch it for truth. This informant, "the Reverend Mr. Peter Angel, minister of Vand-Elvens Gield, on Suderoe," assured his bishop, when he was on a visitation journey, that "in the year 1719, he (being then about twenty years old) saw what is called a merman lying dead on a point of land near the sea, which had been cast ashore by the waves along with several sea-calves (seals), and other dead fish.

The length of this creature was much greater than what has been mentioned of any before, namely, above three fathoms. It was of a dark grey colour all over: in the lower part it was like a fish, and had a tail like that of a porpoise. The face resembled that of a man, with a mouth, forehead, eyes, etc. The nose was flat, and, as it were, pressed down to the face, in which the nostrils were very visible. The breast was not far from the head; the arms seemed to hang to the side, to which they were joined by a thin skin, or membrane. The hands were, to all appearance, like the paws of a sea-calf. The back of this creature was very fat, and a great part of it was cut off, which, with the liver, yielded a large quantity of train-oil." The author then quotes a description by Luke Debes * of a mermaid seen in 1670 at Faroe, westward of Qualboe Eide, by many of the inhabitants, as also by others from different parts of Suderoe. She was close to the shore, and stood there for two hours and a half, and was up to her waist in water. She had long hairs on her head, which hung down to the surface of the water all round about her, and she held a fish in her right hand.

Pontoppidan mentions other instances of similar appearances, and says that the latest he had heard of was of a merman seen in Denmark on the 20th of September, 1723, by three ferrymen who, at some distance from the land, were towing a ship just arrived from the Baltic. Having caught sight of something which looked like a dead body floating on the water, they rowed towards it, and there, resting on their oars, allowed it to drift close to them. It sank, but immediately came to the surface again, and then they saw that it had the appearance of an old man, strong-

* *Feroa Reserata*, or Description of the Feroe Islands. 8vo. Copenhagen, 1673.

limbed, and with broad shoulders, but his arms they could not see. His head was small in proportion to his body, and had short, curled, black hair, which did not reach below his ears; his eyes lay deep in his head, and he had a meagre and pinched face, with a black, coarse beard, that looked as if it had been cut. His skin was coarse, and very full of hair. He stood in the same place for half a quarter of an hour, and was seen above the water down to his breast: at last the men grew apprehensive of some danger, and began to retire; upon which the monster blew up his cheeks, and made a kind of roaring noise, and then dived under water, so that they did not see him any more. One of them, Peter Gunnersen, related (what the others did not observe) that this merman was, about the body and downwards, quite pointed, like a fish. This same Peter Gunnersen likewise deposed that "about twenty years before, as he was in a boat near Kulleor, the place where he was born, he saw a mermaid with long hair and large breasts." He and his two companions were, by command of the king, examined by the burgomaster of Elsineur, Andrew Bussæus, before the privy-councillor, Fridrich von Gram, and their testimony to the above effect was given on their respective oaths.

Brave old Henry Hudson, the sturdy and renowned navigator, who thrice, in three successive years, gave battle to the northern ice, and was each time defeated in his endeavour to discover a north-west or north-east passage to China, though he stamped his name on the title-page of a mighty nation's history, records the following incident: "This evening (June 15th) one of our company, looking overboard, saw a mermaid, and, calling up some of the company to see her, one more of the crew came up, and by that time she was come close to the ship's side, looking earnestly on the men. A little after a sea came and overturned her. From the navel upward, her back and breasts were like a woman's, as they say that saw her; her body as big as one of us, her skin very white, and long hair hanging down behind, of colour black. In her going down they saw her tail, which was like the tail of a porpoise and speckled like a mackarel's. Their names that saw her were Thomas Hilles and Robert Rayner."

Steller, who was a zoologist of some repute, reports having seen in Behrings Straits a strange animal, which he calls a "sea-ape," and in which one might almost recognise Pontoppidan's "Sea-Quoyas-Morrov." It was about five feet long, had sharp and erect ears and large eyes, and on its lips a kind of beard. Its body was thick and round, and it tapered to the tail, which was bifurcated, with the upper lobe longest. It was covered with thick hair, grey on the back, and red on the belly. No feet nor paws were visible. It was full of frolic, and sported in the manner of a monkey, swimming sometimes on one side of the ship and sometimes on the other. It often raised one-third of its body out of the water, and stood upright for a considerable time. It would frequently bring up a sea-plant, not unlike a bottle-gourd, which it would toss about and catch in its mouth, playing numberless fantastic tricks with it.

Somewhat similar accounts have been brought from the Southern Hemisphere, two, at least, of which are worth transcribing.

Captain Colnett, in his 'Voyage to the South Atlantic,' says:—"A very singular circumstance happened off the coast of Chili, in lat. 24° S., which spread some alarm amongst my people, and awakened their superstitious apprehensions. About 8 o'clock in the evening an animal rose alongside the ship, and uttered such shrieks and tones of lamentation, so much like those produced by the female human voice when expressing the deepest distress as to occasion no small degree of alarm among those who first heard it. These cries continued for upwards of three hours, and seemed to increase as the ship sailed from it. I never heard any noise whatever that approached so near those sounds which proceed from the organs of utterance in the human species."

Captain Weddell, in his 'Voyage towards the South Pole' (p. 143), writes that one of his men, having been left ashore on Hall's Island to take care of some produce, heard one night about ten o'clock, after he had lain down to rest, a noise resembling human cries. As daylight does not disappear in those latitudes at the season in which the incident occurred, the sailor rose and searched along the beach, thinking that, possibly, a boat might have been upset, and that some of the crew might be clinging to the detached rocks.

> "Roused by that voice of silver sound,
> From the paved floor he lightly sprung,
> And, glaring with his eyes around,
> Where the fair nymph her tresses wrung," *

guided by occasional sounds, he at length saw an object lying on a rock a dozen yards from the shore, at which he was somewhat frightened. "The face and shoulders appeared of human form and of a reddish colour; over the shoulders hung long green hair; the tail resembled that of a seal, but the extremities of the arms he could not see distinctly."

> "As on the wond'ring youth she smiled,
> Again she raised the melting lay,"*

---

* John Leyden.

for the creature continued to make a musical noise during the two minutes he gazed at it, and, on perceiving him, disappeared in an instant.

The universality of the belief in an animal of combined human and fish-like form is very remarkable. That it exists amongst the Japanese we have evidence in their curious and ingeniously-constructed models which are occasionally brought to this country. I have one of these which is so exactly the counterpart of that which my friend Mr. Frank Buckland described, originally in *Land and Water*, and which forms the subject of a chapter in his 'Curiosities of Natural History,'* that the portrait of the one (Fig. 13) will equally well represent

FIG. 13.—A JAPANESE ARTIFICIAL MERMAID.

the other. The lower half of the body is made of the skin and scales of a fish of the carp family, and fastened on to this, so neatly that it is hardly possible to detect where the joint is made, is a wooden body, the ribs of which are so prominent that the poor mermaid has a miserable and half-starved appearance. The upper part of the body is in the attitude of a Sphinx, leaning upon its elbows and fore-arms. The arms are thin and scraggy, and the fingers attenuated and skeleton-like. The nails are formed of small pieces of

* Third Series, vol. ii. p. 134, 2nd ed.

ivory or bone. The head is like that of a small monkey, and a little wool covers the crown, so thinly and untidily that if the mermaid possessed a crystal mirror she would see the necessity for the vigorous use of her comb of pearl. The teeth are those of some fish—apparently of the cat-fish, (*Anarchicas lupus*). These Japanese artificial mermaids have brought many a dollar into the pockets of Mr. Barnum and other showmen.

Somewhat different in appearance from this, but of the same kind, was an artificial mermaid described in the *Saturday Magazine* of June 4th, 1836. Fig. 14 is a facsimile of the woodcut which accompanied it. This grotesque composition was exhibited in a glass case, some years previously, "in a leading street at the west end" of London. It was constructed "of the skin of the head and shoulders of a monkey, which was attached to the dried skin of a fish of the salmon kind with the head cut off, and the whole was stuffed and highly varnished, the better to deceive the eye." It was said to have been "taken by the crew of a Dutch vessel from on board a native Malacca boat, and from the reverence shown to it, it was supposed to be a representative of one of their idol gods." I am inclined to think that it was of Japanese origin.

FIG. 14.—AN ARTIFICIAL MERMAID, PROBABLY JAPANESE.

Fig. 15 is described in the article above referred to as having been copied from a Japanese drawing, and as being a portrait of one of their deities. Its similarity to one of those of the Assyrians (Fig. 2, page 3) is remarkable. The inscription, however, does not indicate this. The Chinese characters in the centre—"*Nin giyo*"—signify "human fish;" those on the right in Japanese *Hira Kana*, or running-hand, have the same purport, and those on the left, in *Kata Kana*, the characters of the Japanese alphabet, mean "*Ichi hiru ike*"—"one day kept alive." The whole legend seems to pretend that this human fish was actually caught, and kept alive in water for twenty-four hours, but, as the box on which it is inscribed is one of those in which the Japanese showmen keep their toys, it was probably the subject of a "penny peep-show."

We need not travel from our own country to find the belief in mermaids yet existing. It is still credited in the north of Scotland that they inhabit the neighbouring seas: and Dr. Robert Hamilton, F.R.S.E., writing in 1839, expressed emphatically his opinion that there was then as much ignorance on this subject as had prevailed at any former period.*

FIG. 15.—A MERMAID. *From a Japanese picture.*

In the year 1797, Mr. Munro, schoolmaster of Thurso, affirmed that he had seen "a figure like a naked female, sitting on a rock projecting into the sea, at Sandside Head, in the parish of Reay. Its head was covered with long, thick, light-brown hair, flowing down on the shoulders. The forehead was round, the face plump, and the cheeks ruddy. The mouth and lips resembled those of a human being, and the eyes were blue. The arms, fingers, breast,

* Naturalist's Library, Marine Amphibiæ, p. 291.

and abdomen were as large as those of a full-grown female," and, altogether,

> "That sea-nymph's form of pearly light
> Was whiter than the downy spray,
> And round her bosom, heaving bright,
> Her glossy yellow ringlets play." *

"This creature," continued Mr. Munro, "was apparently in the act of combing its hair with its fingers, which seemed to afford it pleasure, and it remained thus occupied during some minutes, when it dropped into the sea." The Dominie

> "saw the maiden there,
> Just as the daylight faded,
> Braiding her locks of gowden hair
> An' singing as she braided," †

but he did not remark whether the fingers were webbed. On the whole he infers that this was a marine animal of which he had a distinct and satisfactory view, and that the portion seen by him bore a narrow resemblance to the human form. But for the dangerous situation it had chosen, and its appearance among the waves, he would have supposed it to be a woman. Twelve years later, several persons observed near the same spot an animal which they also supposed to be a mermaid.

A very remarkable story of this kind is one related by Dr. Robert Hamilton in the volume already referred to, and for the general truth of which he vouches, from his personal knowledge of some of the persons connected with the occurrence. In 1823 it was reported that some fishermen of Yell, one of the Shetland group, had captured a mermaid by its being entangled in their lines. The statement was that

---

* John Leyden.
† The Ettrick Shepherd.

"the animal was about three feet long, the upper part of the body resembling the human, with protuberant mammæ, like a woman; the face, forehead, and neck were short, and resembled those of a monkey; the arms, which were small, were kept folded across the breast; the fingers were distinct, not webbed; a few stiff, long bristles were on the top of the head, extending down to the shoulders, and these it could erect and depress at pleasure, something like a crest. The inferior part of the body was like a fish. The skin was smooth, and of a grey colour. It offered no resistance, nor attempted to bite, but uttered a low, plaintive sound. The crew, six in number, took it within their boat, but, superstition getting the better of curiosity, they carefully disentangled it from the lines and a hook which had accidentally become fastened in its body, and returned it to its native element. It instantly dived, descending in a perpendicular direction." Mr. Edmonston, the original narrator of this incident, was "a well-known and intelligent observer," says Dr. Hamilton, and in a communication made by him to the Professor of Natural History in the Edinburgh University gave the following additional particulars, which he had learned from the skipper and one of the crew of the boat. "They had the animal for three hours within the boat: the body was without scales or hair; it was of a silvery grey colour above, and white below; it was like the human skin; no gills were observed, nor fins on the back or belly. The tail was like that of a dog-fish; the mammæ were about as large as those of a woman; the mouth and lips were very distinct, and resembled the human. Not one of the six men dreamed of a doubt of its being a mermaid, and it could not be suggested that they were influenced by their fears, for the mermaid is not an object of terror to fishermen: it is rather a welcome guest, and danger is apprehended from its experiencing bad treatment." Mr. Edmonston concludes by saying that "the usual resources of scepticism that the seals and other sea-animals appearing under certain circumstances, operating upon an excited imagination, and so producing ocular illusion, cannot avail here. It is quite impossible that six Shetland fishermen could commit such a mistake." It would seem that the narrator demands that his readers shall be silenced, if unconvinced ; but

> "He that complies against his will
> Is of his own opinion still."

This incident is well-attested, and merits respectful and careful consideration ; but I decline to admit any such impossibility of error in observation or description on the part of the fishermen, or the further impossibility of recognising in the animal captured by them one known to naturalists. The particulars given in this instance, and also of the supposed merman seen cast ashore dead in 1719 by the Rev. Peter Angel (p. 22), are sufficiently accurate descriptions of a warm-blooded marine animal, with which the Shetlanders, and probably Mr. Edmonston also, were unacquainted, namely, the rytina, of which I shall have more to say presently ; and these occurrences afford some slight hope that this remarkable beast may not have become extinct in 1768, as has been supposed, but that it may still exist somewhat further south than it was met with by its original describer, Steller.

Turning to Ireland, we find the same credence in the semi-human fish, or fish-tailed human being. In the autumn of 1819 it was affirmed that "a creature appeared on the Irish coast, about the size of a girl ten years of age, with a bosom as prominent as one of sixteen, having a profusion of long dark-brown hair, and full, dark eyes. The hands and arms were formed like those of a man, with a slight web connecting the upper part of the fingers, which were frequently employed in throwing back and dividing the hair. The tail appeared like that of a dolphin." This creature remained basking on the rocks during an hour, in the sight of numbers of people, until frightened by the flash of a musket, when

> "Away she went with a sea-gull's scream,
> And a splash of her saucy tail,"*

for it instantly plunged with a scream into the sea.

From Irish legends we learn that those sea-nereids, the "Merrows," or "Moruachs" came occasionally from the sea, gained the affections of men, and interested themselves in their affairs ; and similar traditions of the "Morgan" (sea-women) and the "Morverch" (sea-daughters) are current in Brittany.

In English poetry the mermaid has been the subject of many charming verses, and Shakspeare alludes to it in his plays no less than six times. The head-quarters of these "daughters of the sea" in England, or of the belief in their existence, are in Cornwall. There the fisherman, many a time and

> "Oft, beneath the silver moon,†
> Has heard, afar, the mermaid sing,"

and has listened, so they say, to

> "The mermaid's sweet sea-soothing lay
> That charmed the dancing waves to sleep."†

---

* Tom Hood. 'The Mermaid at Margate.'
† John Leyden.

Mr. Robert Hunt, F.R.S., in his collection of the traditions and superstitions of old Cornwall,* records several curious legends of the "merrymaids" and "merrymen" (the local name of mermaids), which he had gathered from the fisher-folk and peasants in different parts of that county.

And, in a pleasant article in 'All the Year Round,'† 1865, "A Cornish Vicar"‡ mentions some of the superstitions of the people in his neighbourhood, and the perplexing questions they occasionally put to him. One of his parishioners, an old man named Anthony Cleverdon, but who was popularly known as "Uncle Tony," having been the seventh son of his parents, in direct succession, was looked upon, in consequence, as a soothsayer. This "ancient augur" confided to his pastor many highly efficacious charms and formularies, and, in return, sought for information from him on other subjects. One day he puzzled the parson by a question which so well illustrates the local ideas concerning mermaids, and the sequel of which is, moreover, so humorously related by the vicar, that I venture to quote his own words, as follows:—

"Uncle Tony said to me, 'Sir, there is one thing I want to ask you, if I may be so free, and it is this: why should a merrymaid, that will ride about upon the waters in such terrible storms, and tess from sea to sea in such ruckles as there be upon the coast, why should she never lose her looking-glass and comb?' 'Well, I suppose,' said I, 'that if there are such creatures, Tony, they must wear their looking-glasses and combs fastened on somehow, like fins

---

* 'Romances and Drolls of the West of England.' London: Hotten, 1871.

† Vol. xiii. p. 336.

‡ The "Cornish Vicar" was, evidently, the Rev. Robert Stephen Hawker, M.A., Vicar of Morwenstow, and author of 'Echoes from Old Cornwall,' 'Footprints of Former Men in Cornwall,' etc.

to a fish.' 'See!' said Tony, chuckling with delight, 'what a thing it is to know the Scriptures, like your reverence; I should never have found it out. But there's another point, sir, I should like to know, if you please; I've been bothered about it in my mind hundreds of times. Here be I, that have gone up and down Holacombe cliffs and streams fifty years come next Candlemas, and I've gone and watched the water by moonlight and sunlight, days and nights, on purpose, in rough weather and smooth (even Sundays, too, saving your presence), and my sight as good as most men's, and yet I never could come to see a merrymaid in all my life: how's that, sir?' 'Are you sure, Tony,' I rejoined, 'that there are such things in existence at all?' 'Oh, sir, my old father seen her twice! He was out one night for wreck (my father watched the coast, like most of the old people formerly), and it came to pass that he was down at the duck-pool on the sand at low-water tide, and all to once he heard music in the sea. Well, he croped on behind a rock, like a coastguardsman watching a boat, and got very near the music . . . . and there was the merrymaid, very plain to be seen, swimming about upon the waves like a woman bathing—and singing away. But my father said it was very sad and solemn to hear—more like the tune of a funeral hymn than a Christmas carol, by far—but it was so sweet that it was as much as he could do to hold back from plunging into the tide after her. And he an old man of sixty-seven, with a wife and a houseful of children at home. The second time was down here by Holacombe Pits. He had been looking out for spars—there was a ship breaking up in the Channel—and he saw some one move just at half-tide mark, so he went on very softly, step by step, till he got nigh the place, and there was the merrymaid sitting on a rock, the bootyfullest merrymaid that eye could behold, and she was twisting about her long hair, and dressing it, just like one of our girls getting ready for her sweetheart on the Sabbath-day. The old man made sure he should creep hold of her before ever she found him out, and he had got so near that a couple of paces more and he would have caught her by the hair, as sure as tithe or tax, when, lo and behold, she looked back and glimpsed him! So, in one moment she dived head-foremost off the rock, and then tumbled herself topsy-turvy about in the water, and cast a look at my poor father, and grinned like a seal.'" And a seal it probably was that Tony's "poor father" saw.

What, then, are these mermaids and mermen, a belief in whose existence has prevailed in all ages, and amongst all the nations of the earth? Have they, really, some of the parts and proportions of man, or do they belong to another order of mammals on which credulity and inaccurate observation have bestowed a false character?

Mr. Swainson, a naturalist of deserved eminence, has maintained on purely scientific grounds, that there must exist a marine animal uniting the general form of a fish with that of a man; that by the laws of Nature the natatorial type of the *Quadrumana* is most assuredly wanting, and that, apart from man, a being connecting the seals with the monkeys is required to complete the circle of quadrumanous animals.*

Mr. Gosse † argues that all the characters which Mr. Swainson selects as marking the natatorial type of animals belong to man, and that he being, in his savage state, a great swimmer, is the true aquatic primate, which Mr. Swainson regards as absent. Mr. Gosse admits, however, that "nature

---

* 'Geography and Distribution of Animals.'
† 'Romance of Natural History,' 2nd Series.

has an odd way of mocking at our impossibilities, and" that "it *may be* that green-haired maidens with oary tails, lurk in the ocean caves, and keep mirrors and combs upon their rocky shelves;" and the conclusion he arrives at is that the combined evidence "induces a strong suspicion that the northern seas may hold forms of life as yet uncatalogued by science."

That there are animals in the northern and other seas with which we are unacquainted, is more than probable: discoveries of animals of new species are constantly being made, especially in the life of the deep sea. But I venture to think that the production of an animal at present unknown is quite unnecessary to account for the supposed appearances of mermaids.

We have in the form and habits of the *Phocidæ*, or earless seals, a sufficient interpretation of almost every incident of the kind that has occurred north of the Equator—of those in which protuberant *mammæ* are described, we must presently seek another explanation. The round, plump, expressive face of a seal, the beautiful, limpid eyes, the hand-like fore-paws, the sleek body, tapering towards the flattened hinder fins, which are directed backwards, and spread out in the form of a broad fin, like the tail of a fish, might well give the idea of an animal having the anterior part of its body human and the posterior half piscine.

In the habits of the seals, also, we may trace those of the supposed mermaid, and the more easily the better we are acquainted with them. All seals are fond of leaving the water frequently. They always select the flattest and most shelving rocks which have been covered at high tide, and prefer those that are separated from the mainland. They generally go ashore at half-tide, and invariably lie with their heads towards the water, and seldom more than a yard or two from it. There they will often remain, if undisturbed, for six hours; that is, until the returning tide floats them off the rock. As for the sweet melody, "so melting soft," that must depend much on the ear and musical taste of the listener. I have never heard a seal utter any vocal sounds but a porcine grunt, a plaintive moan, and a pitiful whine. But another habit of the seals has, probably more than anything else, caused them to be mistaken for semi-human beings—namely, that of poising themselves upright in the water with the head and the upper third part of the body above the surface.

One calm sunny morning in August, 1881, a fine schooner-yacht, on board of which I was a guest, was slowly gliding out of the mouth of the river Maas, past the Hook of Holland, into the North Sea, when a seal rose just ahead of us, and assumed the attitude above described. It waited whilst we passed it, inspecting us apparently with the greatest interest; then dived, swam in the direction in which we were sailing, so as to intercept our course, and came up again, sitting upright as before. This it repeated three times, and so easily might it have been taken for a mermaid, that one of the party, who was called on deck to see it, thought, at first, that it was a boy who had swam off from the shore to the vessel on a begging expedition.

Laing, in his account of a voyage to the North, mentions having seen a seal under similar circumstances.

A young seal which was brought from Yarmouth to the Brighton Aquarium in 1873, habitually sat thus, showing his head and a considerable portion of his body out of water. His bath was so shallow in some parts that he was able to touch the bottom, and, with his after-flippers tucked under him, like a lobster's tail, and spread out in front, he would balance himself on his hind quarters, and look inquisitively at everybody, and listen attentively to everything within sight and hearing. When he was satisfied that no one was likely to interfere with him, and that it was unnecessary to be on the alert, he would half-close his beautiful, soft eyes, and either contentedly pat, stroke, and scratch his little fat stomach with his right paw, or flap both of them across his breast in a most ludicrous manner, exactly as a cabman warms the tips of his fingers on a wintry day, by swinging his arms vigorously across his chest, and striking his hands against his body on either side. He was very sensitive to musical sounds, as many dogs are, and when a concert took place in the building a high note from one of the vocalists would cause him to utter a mournful wail, and to dive with a splash that made the water fly, the audience smile, and the singer frown.

Captain Scoresby tells us that he had seen the walrus with its head above water, and in such a position that it required little stretch of imagination to mistake it for a human being, and that on one occasion of this kind the surgeon of his ship actually reported to him that he had seen a man with his head above water.

Peter Gunnersen's merman (p. 24), who "blew up his cheeks and made a kind of roaring noise" before diving, was probably a "bladder-nose" seal. The males of that species have on the head a peculiar pad, which they can dilate at pleasure, and their voice is loud and discordant.

The appearance and behaviour of Steller's "sea-ape," described on p. 25, may, I think, be attributed to one of the eared seals, the so-called sea-lions, or sea-bears. Every one who has seen these animals fed must have noticed the rapidity with which they will dive and swim to any part of their pond where they expect to receive food, and how, like a dog after a pebble, they will keenly watch their keeper's movements, and start in the direction to which he is apparently about to throw a fish, even before the latter has left his hand. This may be seen at the Zoological Gardens, Regent's Park, and, better than anywhere else in Europe, at the Jardin d'Acclimatation, Paris. It would be quite in accordance with their habits that one of these *Otaria* should dive under a ship, and rise above the surface on either side, eagerly surveying those on board, in hope of obtaining food, or from mere curiosity.

The seals and their movements account for so many mermaid stories, that all accounts of sea-women with prominent bosoms were ridiculed and discredited until competent observers recognised in the form and habits of certain aquatic animals met with in the bays and estuaries of the Indian Ocean, the Red Sea, the west coast of Africa, and sub-tropical America, the originals of these "travellers' tales." These were—first, the *manatee*, which is found in the West Indian Islands, Florida, the Gulf of Mexico, and Brazil, and in Africa in the River Congo, Senegambia, and the Mozambique Channel; second, the *dugong*, or *halicore*, which ranges along the east coast of Africa, Southern Asia, the Bornean Archipelago, and Australia; and, third, the *rytina*, seen on Behring's Island in the Kamschatkan Sea by Steller, the Russian zoologist and voyager, in 1741, and which is supposed to have become extinct within twenty-seven years after its discovery, by its having been recklessly and indiscriminately slaughtered.* Then science, in the person of Illeger, made the *amende honorable*, and frankly

* Almost all that is known of the living rytina is from an account published in 1751, in St. Petersburg, by Steller, who was one of an exploring party wrecked on Behring's Island in 1741. During the ten months the crew remained on the island they pursued this easily-captured animal so persistently, for food, that it was all but annihilated at the time. The last one there was killed in 1768.

accepting Jack's introduction to his fish-tailed *innamorata*, classed these three animals together as a sub-order of the animal kingdom, and bestowed on them the name of the *Sirenia*. This was, of course, in allusion to the Sirens of classical mythology, who, in later art, were represented as having the body of a woman above the waist, and that of a fish below, although the lower portion of their body was originally described as being in the form of a bird.

It has been found difficult to determine to which order these *Manatidæ* are most nearly allied. In shape they most closely resemble the whales and seals. But the cetacea are all carnivorous, whereas the manatee and its relatives live entirely on vegetable food. Although, therefore, Dr. J. E. Gray, following Cuvier, classed them with the cetacea in his British Museum catalogue, other anatomists, as Professor Agassiz, Professor Owen, and Dr. Murie, regard their resemblance to the whales as rather superficial than real, and conclude from their organisation and dentition that they ought either to form a group apart or be classed with the pachyderms—the hippopotamus, tapir, etc.—with which they have the nearest affinities, and to which they seem to have been more immediately linked by the now lost genera, *Dinotherium* and *Halitherium*. With the opinion of those last-named authorities I entirely agree. I regard the manatee as exhibiting a wonderful modification and adaptation of the structure of a warm-blooded land animal which enables it to pass its whole life in water, and as a connecting link between the hippopotamus, elephant, etc., on the one side, and the whales and seals on the other.

The *Halitherium* was a Sirenian with which we are only acquainted by its fossil remains found in the Miocene formation of Central and Southern Europe. These indicate that it had short hind limbs, and, consequently, approached more nearly the terrestrial type than either the manatee, the rytina, or the dugong, in which the hind limbs are absent. The two last named tend more than does the manatee to the marine mammals; but there is a strong likeness between these three recent forms. They all have a cylindrical body, like that of a seal, but instead of hind limbs there is in all a broad tail flattened horizontally; and the chief difference in their outward appearance is in the shape of this organ. In the manatee it is rounded, in the dugong forked like that of a whale, in the rytina crescent-shaped. The tail of the *Halitherium* appears to have been shaped somewhat like that of the beaver. The body of the manatee is broader in proportion to its length and depth than that of the dugong. In a paper read before the Royal Society, July 12th, 1821, on a manatee sent to London in spirits by the Duke of Manchester, then Governor of Jamaica, Sir Everard Home remarked of this greater lateral expansion that, as the manatee feeds on plants that grow at the mouths of great rivers, and the dugong upon those met with in the shallows amongst small islands in the Eastern seas, the difference of form would make the manatee more buoyant and better fitted to float in fresh water.

In all the *Manatidæ* the mammæ of the female, which are greatly distended during the period of lactation, are situated very differently from those of the whales, being just beneath the pectoral fins. These fins or paws are much more flexible and free in their movements than those of the cetæ, and are sufficiently prehensile to enable the animal to gather food between the palms or inner surfaces of both, and the female to hold her young one to her breast with one of them. Like the whales, they are warm-blooded mammals, breathing by lungs, and are therefore obliged to come to the surface at frequent intervals for respiration. As they breathe through nostrils at the end of the muzzle, instead of, like most of the whales, through a blow-hole on the top of the head, their habit is to rise, sometimes vertically, in the water, with the head and fore part of the body exposed above the surface, and often to remain in this position for some minutes. When seen thus, with head and breast bare, and clasping its young one to its body, the female presents a certain re-

FIG. 16.—THE DUGONG. *From Sir J. Emerson Tennent's 'Ceylon.'*

semblance to a woman from the waist upward. When approached or disturbed it dives; the tail and hinder portion of the body come into view, and we see that if there was little of the "*mulier formosa superne*," at any rate "*desinit in piscem*." The manatee has thence been called by the Spaniards and Portuguese the "woman-fish," and by the Dutch the "manetje," or mannikin. The dugong, having the muzzle bristly, is named by the latter the "baard-manetje," or "little bearded man." There are no bristles or whiskers on the muzzle of the manatee; all the portraits of it in which these are shown are in that respect erroneous. The origin of the word "manatee" has by some been traced to the Spanish, as indicating "an animal with hands." On the west coast of Africa it is called by the natives "Ne-hoo-le." By old writers it was described as the "sea-cow." Gesner depicts it in the act of bellowing; and Mr. Bates, in his work, "The Naturalist on the Amazon," says that its voice is something like the bellowing of an ox. The Florida "crackers" or "mean whites," make the same statement. Although I have had opportunities of prolonged observation of it in captivity, I have not heard it give utterance to any sound—not even a grunt —and Mr. Bartlett, of the Zoological Gardens, tells me that his experience of it is the same. His son, Mr. Clarence Bartlett, says that a young one he had in Surinam used to make a feeble cry, or bleat, very much like the voice of a young seal. This is the only sound he ever heard from a manatee.[*]

I believe the dugong to be more especially the animal referred to by Ælian as the semi-human whale, and that which has led to this group having been supposed by southern voyagers to be aquatic human beings. In the first place, the dugong is a denizen of the sea, whereas the manatee is chiefly found in rivers and fresh-water lagoons; and secondly, the dugong accords with Ælian's description of the creature with a woman's face in that it has "prickles instead of hairs," whilst the manatee has no such stiff bristles.

In the case of either of these two animals being mistaken

---

[*] For a full description of the habits of this animal in captivity, see an article by the present writer in the 'Leisure Hour' of September 28, 1878; from which the illustration, Fig. 17, is borrowed by the kind consent of the Editor of that publication.

for a mermaid, however, "distance" must "lend enchantment to the view," and a sailor must be very impressible and imaginative who, even after having been deprived for many months of the pleasure of females' society, could be allured by the charms of a bristly-muzzled dugong, or

FIG. 17.—THE MANATEE. ITS USUAL POSITION.

mistake the snorting of a wallowing manatee for the lovesong of a beauteous sea-maiden.

Unfortunately both the dugong and the manatee are being hunted to extinction.

The flesh of the manatee is considered a great delicacy.

Humboldt compares it with ham. Unlike that of the whales, which is of a deep and dark red hue, it is as white as veal, and, it is said, tastes very like it. It is remarkable for retaining its freshness much longer than other meat, which in a tropical climate generally putrefies in twenty-eight hours. It is therefore well adapted for pickling, as the salt has time to penetrate the flesh before it is tainted. The Catholic clergy of South America do not object to its being eaten on fast days, on the supposition that, with whales, seals, and other aquatic mammals, it may be liberally regarded as "fish." The "Indians" of the Amazon and Orinoco are so fond of it that they will spend many days, if necessary, in hunting for a manatee, and having killed one will cut it into slabs and slices on the spot, and cook these on stakes thrust into the ground aslant over a great fire, and heavily gorge themselves as long as the provision lasts. The milk of this animal is said to be rich and good, and the skin is valuable for its toughness, and is much in request for making leathern articles in which great strength and durability are required. The tail contains a great deal of oil, which is believed to be extremely nutritious, and has also the property of not becoming rancid. Unhappily for the dugong, its oil is in similarly high repute, and is greatly preferred as a nutrient medicine to cod-liver oil. As its flesh also is much esteemed, it is so persistently hunted on the Australian coasts that it will probably soon become extinct, like the rytina of Steller. The same fate apparently awaits the manatee, which is becoming perceptibly more and more scarce.

I fear that before many years have elapsed the Sirens of the Naturalist will have disappeared from our earth, before the advance of civilization, as completely as the fables and superstitions with which they have been connected, before the increase of knowledge; and that the mermaid of fact will have become as much a creature of the past as the mermaid of fiction. With regard to the latter—the Siren of the poets,—the water-maiden of the pearly comb, the crystal mirror, and the sea-green tresses,—there are few persons I suppose, at the present day who would not be content to be classed with Banks, the fine old naturalist and formerly ship-mate of Captain Cook. Sir Humphry Davy in his *Salmonia* relates an anecdote of a baronet, a profound believer in these fish-tailed ladies, who on hearing some one praise very highly Sir Joseph Banks, said that " Sir Joseph was an excellent man, but he had his prejudices—he did not believe in the mermaid." I confess to having a similar " prejudice ; " and am willing to adopt the further remark of Sir Humphry Davy :—" I am too much of the school of Izaac Walton to talk of impossibility. It doubtless might please God to make a mermaid, but I don't believe God ever did make one."

THE LERNEAN HYDRA.

THE mystery of the Kraken, of which I treated in a companion volume to the present, recently published, is not difficult to unravel. The clue to it is plain, and when properly taken up is as easily unwound, to arrive at the truth, as a cocoon of silk, to get at the chrysalis within it. It was a boorish exaggeration, a legend of ignorance, superstition, and wonder. But when such a skein of facts has passed through the hands of the poets, it is sure to be found in a much more intricate tangle ; and many a knot of pure invention may have to be cut before it is made clear.

Nevertheless, we shall be able to discern that more than one of the most famous and hideous monsters of old classical lore originated, like the Kraken, in a knowledge by their authors of the form and habits of those strange sea-creatures, the head-footed mollusks. There can be little doubt that the octopus was the model from which the old poets and artists formed their ideas, and drew their pictures of the Lernean Hydra, whose heads grew again when cut off by Hercules ; and also of the monster Scylla, who, with six heads and six long writhing necks, snatched men off the decks of passing ships and devoured them in the recesses of her gloomy cavern.

Of the Hydra Diodorus relates that it had a hundred heads ; Simonides says fifty ; but the generally received opinion was that of Apollodorus, Hyginus, and others, that it had only nine.

Apoliodorus of Athens, son of Asclepiades, who wrote in stiff, quaint Greek about 120 B.C., gives in his 'Bibliotheca' (book ii. chapter 5, section 2) the following account of the many-headed monster. "This Hydra," he says, "nourished in the marshes of Lerne, went forth into the open country and destroyed the herds of the land. It had a huge body and nine heads, eight mortal, but the ninth immortal. Having mounted his chariot, which was driven by Iolaus, Hercules got to Lerne and stopped his horses. Finding the Hydra on a certain raised ground near the source of the Amymon, where its lair was, he made it come out by pelting it with burning missiles. He seized and stopped it, but having twisted itself round one of his feet, it struggled with him. He broke its head with his club: but that was useless; for when one head was broken two sprang up, and a huge crab helped the Hydra by biting the foot of Hercules. This he killed, and called Iolaus, who, setting on fire part of the adjoining forest, burned with torches the germs of the growing heads, and stopped their development. Having thus out-manœuvred the growing heads, he cut off the immortal head, buried it, and put a heavy stone upon it, beside the road going from Lerne to Eleonta, and having opened the Hydra, dipped his arrows in its gall."

If we wish to find in nature the counterpart of this Hydra, we must seek, firstly, for an animal with eight outgrowths from its trunk, which it can develop afresh, or replace by new ones, in case of any or all of them being amputated or injured. We must also show that this animal, so strange in form and possessing such remarkable attributes, was well known in the locality where the legend was believed. We have it in the octopus, which abounded in the Mediterranean and Ægean seas, and whose eight prehensile arms, or tentacles, spring from its central body, the immortal head, and which, if lost or mutilated by misadventure, are capable of reproduction.

That a knowledge of the octopus existed at a very early period of man's history we have abundant evidence. The ancient Egyptians figured it amongst their hieroglyphics, and an interesting proof that they were also acquainted with other cephalopods was given to me by the late Mr. E. W. Cooke, R.A. Whilst on a trip up the Nile, in January, 1875, he visited the temple of Bayr-el-Bahree, Thebes (date 1700 B.C.), the entrance to which had been deeply buried beneath the light, wind-drifted sand, accu-

FIG. 18.—FIGURE OF A CALAMARY. *From the temple of Bayr-el-Bahree.*

mulated during many centuries. By order of the Khedive, access had just at that time been obtained to its interior, by the excavation and removal of this deep deposit, and, amongst the hieroglyphics on the walls, were found, between the zig-zag lines which represent water, figures of various fishes, copies of which Mr. Cooke kindly gave me, and which are so accurately portrayed as to be easily identified. With them was the outline of a squid fourteen inches long, a figure of which, from Mr. Cooke's drawing, is here shown. As this temple is five hundred miles from the delta of the Nile, it is remarkable that nearly all the fishes there represented are of marine species.

That the octopus was a familiar object with the ancient Greeks, we know by the frequency with which its portrait is found on their coins, gems, and ornaments. Aldrovandus describes "very ancient coins" found at Syracuse and Tarentum bearing the figure of an octopus. He says the Syracusans had two coins, one of bronze, the other of gold, both of which had an octopus alone on one

FIG. 19.—FIGURE OF AN OCTOPUS ON A GOLD ORNAMENT, FOUND BY DR. SCHLIEMANN AT MYCENÆ.

side. On the reverse of the bronze one was a veiled female face in profile, with the inscription ΣΥΡΑ. I have one of these bronze Syracusan coins; it was kindly given to me, some years ago, by my friend Dr. John Millar, F.L.S. The octopus is really well depicted. On the gold coin the female head was differently veiled, and at the back of the neck was a fish. The inscription on this coin was

ΣΥΡΑΚΟΣΙΩΝ. Goltzius was of the opinion that the head was that of Arethusa. The coins found at Tarentum had on one side a figure of Neptune seated on a dolphin, and holding an octopus in one hand and a trident in the other.

Lerne, or Lerna, the reputed home of the Hydra, was a port of Southern Greece, situated at the head of the Gulf of Nauplia, and between the existing towns of Argos and Tripolitza. Within a few miles of it was Mycenæ; and it is remarkable that Dr. Schliemann, during his excavations

FIG. 20.—GOLDEN ORNAMENT IN FORM OF AN OCTOPUS, FOUND BY DR. SCHLIEMANN AT MYCENÆ.

there in 1876, found in a tomb a gold plate, or button, two and a half inches in diameter (Fig. 19), on which is figured an octopus, the eight arms of which are converted into spirals, the head and the two eyes being distinctly visible. In another sepulchre he discovered fifty-three golden models of the octopus (Fig 20), all exactly alike, and apparently cast in the same mould. The arms are very naturally carved. By the kindness of Mr. Murray, his publisher, I am enabled to give illustrations of these and two other handsome ornaments.

Having ascertained that the octopus was a familiar object in the very locality where the combat between Hercules and the Hydra is supposed to have taken place, let us compare the animal as it exists with the monstrous offspring of Typhon and Echidna.

It is a not uncommon occurrence that when an octopus is caught it is found to have one or more of its arms shorter than the rest, and showing marks of having been amputated, and of the formation of a new growth from the old cicatrix. Several such specimens were brought to the Brighton Aquarium whilst I had charge of its Natural History

FIG. 21.   FIG. 22.

FIGURES OF THE OCTOPUS ON GOLD ORNAMENTS FOUND BY
DR. SCHLIEMANN AT MYCENÆ.

Department. One of them was particularly interesting. Two of its arms had evidently been bitten off about four inches from the base: and out from the end of each healed stump (which in proportion to the length of the limb was as if a man's arm had been amputated halfway between the shoulder and the elbow), grew a slender little piece of newly-formed arm, about as large as a lady's stiletto, or a small button-hook—in fact just the equivalent of worthy Captain Cuttle's iron hook, which did duty for his lost hand. It was an illustrative example of the commencement of the repair and restoration of mutilated limbs.

This mutilation is so common in some localities, that

Professor Steenstrup says * that almost every octopus he has examined has had one or two arms reproduced; and that he has seen females in which all the eight arms had been lost, but were more or less restored. He also mentions a male in which this was the case as to seven of its arms. He adds that whilst the *Octopoda* possess the power of reproducing with great facility and rapidity their arms, which are exposed to so many enemies, the *Decapoda*—the *Sepiidæ* and Squids—appear to be incapable of thus repairing and replacing accidental injuries. This is entirely in accord with my own observations.

This reparative power is possessed by some other animals, of which the starfishes and crustacea are the most familiar instances. In the case of the lobster or crab, however, the only joint from which new growth can start is that connected with the body, so that if a limb be injured in any part, the whole of it must be got rid of, and the animal has, therefore, the power of casting it off at will. The octopus, on the contrary, is incapable of voluntary dismemberment, but reproduces the lost portion of an injured arm, as an out-growth from the old stump.

The ancients were well acquainted with this reparative faculty of the octopus: but of course the simple fact was insufficient for an imaginative people: and they therefore embellished it with some fancies of their own. There lingers still amongst the fishermen of the Mediterranean a very old belief that the octopus when pushed by hunger will gnaw and devour portions of its arms. Aristotle knew of this belief, and positively contradicted it; but a fallacy once planted is hard to eradicate. You may cut it down, and apparently destroy it, root and branch, but its seeds are scattered abroad, and spring up elsewhere, and in un-

* Ann. and Mag. Nat. Hist. August, 1857.

expected places. Accordingly, we find Oppian, more than five centuries later, disseminating the same old notion, and comparing this habit of the animal with that of the bear obtaining nutriment from his paws by sucking them during his hybernation.

> "When wintry skies o'er the black ocean frown,
> And clouds hang low with ripen'd storms o'ergrown,
> Close in the shelter of some vaulted cave
> The soft-skinn'd prekes* their porous bodies save.
> But forc'd by want, while rougher seas they dread,
> On their own feet, necessitous, are fed.
> But when returning spring serenes the skies,
> Nature the growing parts anew supplies.
> Again on breezy sands the roamers creep,
> Twine to the rocks, or paddle in the deep.
> Doubtless the God whose will commands the seas,
> Whom liquid worlds and wat'ry natives please,
> Has taught the fish by tedious wants opprest
> Life to preserve and be himself the feast.

The fact is, that the larger predatory fishes regard an octopus as very acceptable food, and there is no better bait for many of them than a portion of one of its arms. Some of the cetacea also are very fond of them, and whalers have often reported that when a "fish" (as they call it) is struck it disgorges the contents of its stomach, amongst which they have noticed parts of the arms of cuttles which, judging from the size of their limbs, must have been very large specimens. The food of the sperm whale consists largely of the gregarious squids, and the presence in spermaceti of their undigested beaks is accepted as a test of its being genuine. That old fish-

---

* The octopus is still called the "preke" in some parts of England, notably in Sussex. The translation of Oppian's 'Halieutics,' from which this passage and others are quoted is that by Messrs. Jones and Diaper, of Baliol College, Oxford, and was published in 1722.

reptile, the Ichthyosaurus, also, preyed upon them; and portions of the horny rings of their suckers were discovered in its coprolites by Dean Buckland. Amongst the worst enemies of the octopus is the conger. They are both rock-dwellers, and if the voracious fish come upon his cephalopod neighbour unseen, he makes a meal of him, or, failing to drag him from his hold, bites off as much of one or two of his arms as he can conveniently obtain. The conger, therefore, is generally the author of the injury which the octopus has been unfairly accused of inflicting on itself.

Continuing our comparison with the hydra, we have in the octopus an animal capable of quitting its rocky lurking-place in the sea, and going on a buccaneering expedition on dry land. Many incidents have been related in connection with this; but I can attest it from my own observation. I have seen an octopus travel over the floor of a room at a very fair rate of speed, toppling and sprawling along in its own ungainly fashion; and in May, 1873, we had one at the Brighton Aquarium which used regularly every night to quit its tank, and make its way along the wall to another tank at some distance from it, in which were some young lump-fishes. Day after day, one of these was missing, until, at last, the marauder was discovered. Many days elapsed, however, before he was detected, for after helping himself to, and devouring a young "lump-sucker," he demurely returned before daylight to his own quarters.

Of this habit of the octopus the ancients were, also, fully aware. Aristotle wrote that it left the water and walked in stony places, and Pliny and Ælian related tales of this animal stealing barrels of salt fish from the wharves, and crushing their staves to get at the contents. An octopus that could do this would be as formidable a predatory monster as the Lernean Hydra, which had the evil reputation of devouring the Peloponnesian cattle.

Whoever first described the counter-attack of the Hydra on Hercules must have had the octopus in his thoughts. " It twisted itself round one of his feet "—exactly that which an octopus would do.

Finally, according to the legend, Hercules dipped his arrow-heads in the gall of the Hydra, and, from its poisonous nature, all the wounds he inflicted with them upon his

FIG. 23.—HERCULES SLAYING THE LERNEAN HYDRA.
From Smith's 'Classical Dictionary.'

enemies proved fatal. It is worthy of notice that the ancients attributed to the octopus the possession of a similarly venomous secretion. Thus Oppian writes :

"The crawling preke a deadly juice contains
Injected poison fires the wounded veins."

The accompanying illustration (Fig. 23) of Hercules slaying the Hydra is taken from a marble tablet in the Vatican. It will be immediately seen how closely the Hydra, as there depicted, resembles an octopus. The body is elongated, but the eight necks with small heads on them bear about the same proportion to the body as the arms to the body of an octopus.

The Reverend James Spence, in his 'Polymetis,' published in 1755, gives a figure, almost the counterpart of this, copied from an antique gem, a carnelian, in the collection of the Grand Duke of Tuscany at Florence. Only seven necks of the hydra are, however, there visible, and there are two coils in the elongated body. On the upper part are two spots which have been supposed to represent breasts. This was probably intended by the artificer; but that the idea originated from a duplication of the syphon tube is evident from the figures (Figs. 21, 22) of the octopus on the smaller gold ornaments found by Dr. Schliemann at Mycenæ. In the same work is also an engraving from a picture in the Vatican Virgil, entitled 'The River, or Hateful Passage into the Kingdom of Ades,' wherein an octopus—hydra, of which only six heads and necks are shown, is one of the monsters called by the author "Terrors of the Imagination."

SCYLLA AND CHARYBDIS.

In the description given by Homer, in the twelfth book of the 'Odyssey,' of the unfortunate nymph Scylla, transformed by the arts of Circe into a frightful monster, the same typical idea as in the case of the Hydra is perceptible. The lurking octopus, having its lair in the cranny of a rock, watching in ambush for passing prey, seizing anything coming within its reach with one or more of its prehensile arms, even brandishing these fear-inspiring weapons out of water in a threatening manner, and known in some localities to be dangerous to boats and their occupants, is transformed into a many-headed sea monster, seizing in its mouths, instead of by the adhesive suckers of its numerous arms, the helpless sailors from passing vessels, and devouring them in the abysses of its cavernous den.

Circe, prophesying to Ulysses the dangers he had still to encounter, warned him especially of Scylla and Charybdis, within the power of one of whom he must fall in passing through the narrow strait (between Italy and Sicily) where they had their horrid abode. Describing the lofty rock of Scylla, she tells him:

> "Full in the centre of this rock displayed
> A yawning cavern casts a dreadful shade,
> Nor the fleet arrow from the twanging bow
> Sent with full force, could reach the depth below.
> Wide to the west the horrid gulf extends,
> And the dire passage down to hell descends.

> O fly the dreadful sight! expand thy sails,
> Ply the strong oar, and catch the nimble gales;
> Here Scylla bellows from her dire abodes;
> Tremendous pest! abhorred by man and gods!
> Hideous her voice, and with less terrors roar
> The whelps of lions in the midnight hour.
> Twelve feet deformed and foul the fiend dispreads;
> Six horrid necks she rears, and six terrific heads;
> * * * * * *
> When stung with hunger she embroils the flood,
> The sea-dog and the dolphin are her food;
> She makes the huge leviathan her prey,
> And all the monsters of the wat'ry way;
> The swiftest racer of the azure plain
> Here fills her sails and spreads her oars in vain;
> Fell Scylla rises, in her fury roars,
> At once six mouths expands, at once six men devours." *

Circe then describes the perils of the whirling waters of Charybdis as still more dreadful; and, admonishing Ulysses that once in her power all must perish, she advises him to choose the lesser of the two evils, and to

> "shun the horrid gulf, by Scylla fly;
> 'Tis better six to lose than all to die."

Ulysses continues his voyage; and as his ship enters the ominous strait,

> "Struck with despair, with trembling hearts we viewed
> The yawning dungeon, and the tumbling flood;
> When, lo! fierce Scylla stooped to seize her prey,
> Stretched her dire jaws, and swept six men away.
> Chiefs of renown! loud echoing shrieks arise;
> I turn, and view them quivering in the skies;
> They call, and aid, with outstretched arms, implore,
> In vain they call! those arms are stretched no more.
> As from some rock that overhangs the flood,
> The silent fisher casts th' insidious food;

---

* Homer's 'Odyssey,' Pope's Translation, Book XII.

With fraudful care he waits the finny prize,
And sudden lifts it quivering to the skies;
So the foul monster lifts her prey on high,
So pant the wretches, struggling in the sky;
In the wide dungeon she devours her food,
And the flesh trembles while she churns the blood."

THE "SPOUTING" OF WHALES.

ONE of the sea-fallacies still generally believed, and accepted as true, is that whales take in water by the mouth, and eject it from the spiracle, or blow-hole.

The popular ideas on this subject are still those which existed hundreds of years ago, and which are expressed by Oppian in two passages in his 'Halieutics':

> "Uncouth the sight when they in dreadful play
> Discharge their nostrils and refund a sea,"

and

> "While noisy fin-fish let their fountains fly
> And spout the curling torrent to the sky."

Eminent zoologists and intelligent observers, who have had full opportunities of obtaining practical knowledge of the habits of these great marine mammals, have forcibly combated and repeatedly contradicted this erroneous idea; but their sensible remarks have been read by few, in comparison with the numbers of those to whom a wrong impression has been conveyed by sensational pictures in which whales are represented *with their heads above the surface,* and throwing up from their nostrils columns of water, like the fountains in Trafalgar Square. One can hardly be surprised that the old writers on Natural History were unacquainted with the real composition of the whale's "spout." Those of them who sought for any original information on marine zoology, obtained it chiefly from uninstructed and superstitious fishermen; but they generally contented themselves with diligent compilation, and thus copied and transmitted the errors of their predecessors, with the addition of some slight embellishments of their own. Accordingly, we find Olaus Magnus [*] describing, as follows, the *Physeter*, or, as his translator, Streater, calls it, the *Whirlpool*. " The *Physeter* or *Pristis*," he says, " is a kind of whale, two hundred cubits long, and is very cruel. For, to the danger of seamen, he will sometimes raise himself above the sail-yards, and casts such floods of waters above his head, which he had sucked in, that with a cloud of them he will often sink the strongest ships, or expose the mariners to extreme danger. This beast hath also a large round mouth, like a lamprey, whereby he sucks in his meat or water, and by his weight cast upon the fore or hinder deck, he sinks and drowns a ship."

Figures 24 and 25 (p. 64) are facsimiles of the illustrations which accompany the above description. It will be seen that, in the first, the *Physeter* is depicted as uprearing a maned neck and head, like that of a fabled dragon ; whilst in Fig. 25 it is shown as a whale flinging itself on board a ship, which is sinking under its ponderous weight. In both, torrents of water are issuing from its head, and it is evident that they are merely exaggerated misrepresentations of the " spouting " of whales.

Gesner copies many of Olaus Magnus's illustrations, and improves upon Fig. 25 by putting a numerous crew on board the ship. The unfortunate sailors are depicted in every attitude of terror and despair, and seem to be incapacitated from any attempt to save themselves by the flood of water which the whale is deliberately pouring upon them from its blow-holes.

[*] 'Historia de Gentibus Septentrionalibus,' lib. xxi. cap. vi. A.D. 1555.

FIG. 24.—THE PHYSETER INUNDATING A SHIP. *After Olaus Magnus.*

These old pictures appear, no doubt, ridiculous, but they are, really, very little more absurd and untrue to nature than many of those which disfigure some otherwise useful books on Natural History of the present day. I could

FIG. 25.—A WHALE POURING WATER INTO A SHIP FROM ITS BLOW-HOLE. *After Olaus Magnus.*

refer to several, in which whales are represented as spouting from their blow-holes one or more columns of water, which, after ascending skyward to a considerable distance, fall

FIG. 26.—SPERM WHALES SPOUTING.

over gracefully as if issuing from the nozzle of an ornamental fountain. I select one from amongst them (Fig. 26), not with any disrespect for the artist, author, or publisher of the work from which it is taken, but because, whilst it shows correctly the position of the blow-hole of the sperm whale, it also exhibits exactly that which I wish to confute. The publishers of the valuable work in which this picture appeared have generously consented to my reproducing it here.

When, in describing, in 1877, the White Whale then exhibited at the Westminster Aquarium, I said that whales do not spout water out of their blow-holes, and that the idea that they do so is a popular error, the statement was so contrary to generally-accepted notions that I was not surprised by receiving more than one letter on the subject. One very reasonable suggestion made to me was that, although the lesser whales, such as the porpoises, which I had had opportunities of watching in confinement at Brighton for two years, and the *Beluga*, which had been observed for a similar period at the New York Aquarium, and also at Westminster, did not "spout," the respiratory apparatus of the larger whales might be so modified as to permit them to do so. Let us consider the construction of the breathing apparatus which would have to be thus modified, as shown in the porpoise.

In the first place, there is a pair of lungs as perfect as those of any land mammal, fitted to receive air, and to bring the hot blood into contact with the air, that it may absorb the oxygen of the air, and so be purified. But this air cannot well be breathed through the mouth of an animal which has to take its food from and in water; so it has to be inhaled only by the nostrils. If these were situated as they are in land mammals, near the extremity of the nose, the porpoise would be obliged to stop when pursuing its prey, or, escaping from its enemies, to put the tip of its nose above the surface of the water every time it required to breathe. A much more convenient arrangement has, therefore, been provided for it, and for almost all whales, by which that difficulty is removed. Instead of running along the bones of the nose, the nostrils are placed on the top of the head, and the windpipe is turned up to them without having any connection with the palate. The upper jaw is quite solid. Thus the mouth is solely devoted to the reception of food, and the animal is enabled to continue its course when swimming, however rapidly, by rising obliquely to the surface, and exposing the top of its head above it. On the blow-hole being opened, the air, from which the oxygen has been absorbed, is expelled in a sudden puff, another supply is instantaneously inhaled, and rushes into the lungs with extreme velocity, and then the porpoise can either descend into the depths, or remain with its spiracle exposed to the air, as it may prefer. In this act of breathing the spiracle is normally brought above the water, the breath escapes, and the immediate inhalation is effected almost in silence. But frequently, and in some whales habitually, the blow-hole is opened just below the surface, and then the outrush of air causes a splash upwards of the water overlying it.

I may here mention that I have frequently seen the porpoises at the Brighton Aquarium lying asleep at the surface, with the blow-hole exposed above it, breathing automatically, and without conscious effort. Aristotle was acquainted with this habit of the cetacea 2,200 years ago, for he wrote : "They sleep with the blow-hole, their organ of respiration, elevated above the water."

The apparatus for closing the blow-hole, so that not a drop of water shall enter the windpipe, even under great pressure, is a beautiful contrivance, complex in its structure, yet most simple in its working. The external aperture is covered by a continuation of the skin, locally thickened, and connected with a conical stopper, of a texture as tough as india-rubber, which fits perfectly into a cone or funnel formed by the extremity of the windpipe, and closes more and more firmly as the pressure upon it is increased. Whilst the orifice is thus guarded, the lower end of the tube is surrounded by a strong compressing muscle, which clasps also the glottis, and thus the passage from the blow-hole to the lungs is completely stopped.

There is nothing in this which indicates the possibility of the spouting of water from the nostrils; but as assertions that water had been seen to issue from them were positive and persistent, anatomists seem to have felt themselves obliged to try to account for it somehow. Accordingly the theory was propounded by F. Cuvier that the water taken into the mouth is reserved in two pouches (one on each side), until the whale rises to blow, when, the gullet being closed, it is forced by the action of the tongue and jaws through the nasal passages, somewhat as a smoker occasionally expels the smoke of his cigar through his nostrils. Although these pouches, or sacs analogous to them, are found at the base of the nostrils of the horse, tapir, etc.,—animals which do not "spout" from the nostrils water taken in by the mouth—the explanation was accepted for a time.

Mr. Bell held this opinion when the first edition of his 'British Quadrupeds' was published in 1837, but before the issue of the second edition, in 1874, he had found reasons for taking a different view of the matter; and, under the advice of his judicious editors, Mr. Alston, and Professor Flower (the latter of whom supervised the proofs of the chapters on the Cetacea) his sanction of the illusion was withdrawn as follows:—"The results of more recent and careful observations, amongst which we may notice those of Bennett, Von Baer, Sars and Burmeister, are directly opposed to the statement that water is thus ejected ; and there can now be no doubt that the appearance which has given rise to the idea is caused by the moisture with which the expelled breath is supercharged, which condenses at once in the cold outer air, and forms a cloud or column of white vapour. It is possible indeed that if the animal begins to 'blow' before its head is actually at the surface, the force of the rushing air may drive up some little spray along with it, but this is quite different from the notion that water is really expelled from the nasal passages. We may add that on the only occasion when we ourselves witnessed the 'spouting' of a large whale we were much struck with its resemblance to the column of white spray which is dashed up by the ricochetting ball fired from one of the great guns of a man-of-war."

The simile is admirable, and nothing could better describe the appearance of a whale's "spout"; but, in the previous portion of the passage (except with reference to the sperm whale, the nostrils of which are not on the top of the head), I think sufficient importance is not conceded to the volume of water propelled into the air by the outrush of breath from the submerged blow-hole. I do not know how many cubic feet of air the lungs of a great whale are capable of containing, but the quantity is sufficient to force up to a height of several feet the water above the valve when the latter is opened, not only in "some little spray," but, for some distance in a good solid jet—enough, in fact, to give the appearance of its actually issuing from the blow-hole, and to account for the erroneous belief of sailors that it does so. It must be remembered that the escape of air is not by a prolonged wheeze, but by a sudden blast, and thus when the spiracle is opened just beneath the surface, an instant before it is uncovered to take in a fresh supply of air, the water above its orifice is thrown up as by a slight subaqueous explosion, or as by the momentary opening under water of the safety-valve of a steam boiler. Some idea of the force and volume of the blast of air from the lungs of even the common porpoise may be formed when I mention that one of the porpoises at the Brighton Aquarium, happening to open its spiracle just beneath an illuminating gas jet fixed over its tank, blew out the light.

In the sperm whale the nostrils are placed near the extremity of the nose, and therefore this whale has to raise its snout above the surface when it requires to breathe; but instead of this being necessary, as in the case of the porpoise twice or thrice in a minute, the sperm whale only rises to "blow" at intervals of from an hour to an hour and twenty minutes. Mr. Beale says* that in a large bull sperm whale the time consumed in making one expiration and one inspiration is ten seconds, during six of which the nostril is beneath the surface of the water—the expiration occupying three seconds, and the inspiration one second. At each breathing time this whale makes from sixty to seventy expirations, and remains, therefore, at the surface ten or eleven minutes, and then, raising its tail, it descends perpendicularly, head first. In different individuals the time required for performing these several acts varies; but in each they are minutely regular, and this well-known regularity is of considerable use to the fishers, for when a whaler has once noticed the periods of any particular whale which is not alarmed, he knows to a minute when to expect it to come to the surface, and how long it will remain there. The "spout" of the sperm whale differs much from that of other whales. Unlike, for instance, the straight perpen-

* 'Natural History of the Sperm Whale.' Van Voorst, 1839.

dicular twin jets of the "right whale," the single, forward-slanting "spout" of the sperm whale presents a thick curled bush of white mist. Each whale has a different mode and time of breathing, and the form of the "spout" differs accordingly.

It is said that the blowing of the *Beluga*, or "White Whale," is not unmusical at sea, and that when it takes place under water it often makes a peculiar sound which might be mistaken for the whistling of a bird. Hence is derived one of the names given to this whale by sailors—the "Sea-canary." Though I have had opportunities of attentively watching the breathing and other actions in captivity of two specimens of this whale I have never been able to detect the sound alluded to.

Besides the opinions cited by Mr. Bell concerning whales spouting water from their blow-holes, we have other evidence which is most clear and definite, and which ought to be convincing.

We will take first that of Mr. Beale, who as surgeon on board the "Kent" and "Sarah and Elizabeth," South Sea whalers, passed several seasons amongst sperm whales. He says :—" I can truly say when I find myself in opposition to these old and received notions, that out of the thousands of sperm whales which I have seen during my wanderings in the South and North Pacific Oceans, I have never observed one of them to eject a column of water from the nostril. I have seen them at a distance, and I have been within a few yards of several hundreds of them, and I never saw water pass from the spout-hole. But the column of thick and dense vapour which is certainly ejected is exceedingly likely to mislead the judgment of the casual observer in these matters ; and this column does indeed appear very much like a jet of water when seen at the distance of one or two miles on a clear day, because of the condensation of the vapour which takes place the moment it escapes from the nostril, and its consequent opacity, which makes it appear of a white colour, and which is not observed when the whale is close to the spectator. It then appears only like a jet of white steam. The only water in addition is the small quantity that may be lodged in the external fissure of the spout hole, when the animal raises it above the surface to breathe, and which is blown up into the air with the 'spout,' and may probably assist in condensing the vapour of which it is formed. . . . I have been also very close to the *Balæna mysticetus* (the Greenland, or Right whale) when it has been feeding and breathing, and yet I never saw even that animal differ in the latter respect from the sperm whale in the nature of the spout. . . . If the weather is fine and clear, and there is a gentle breeze at the time, the spout may be seen from the masthead of a moderate-sized vessel at the distance of four or five miles."

Captain Scoresby, who was a veteran and successful whaler, a good zoologist, and a highly intelligent observer, says:—" A moist vapour mixed with mucus is discharged from the nostrils when the animal breathes; but no water accompanies it unless an expiration of the breath be made under the surface."

Dr. Robert Brown, who communicated to the Zoological Society, in May, 1868, a valuable series of observations on the mammals of Greenland, made during his voyages to the Spitzbergen, Iceland, and Jan Mayen Seas, and along the eastern and western shores of Davis's Strait and Baffin's Bay to near the mouth of Smith's Sound, remarks, in a chapter on the Right whale (*Balæna mysticetus*):—" The 'blowing,' so familiar a feature of the *Cetacea*, but especially of the *Mysticetus* is, quite analogous to the breathing of the higher mammals, and the blow-holes are the homologues of the nostrils. It is most erroneously stated that the whale ejects water from the blow-holes. I have been many times only a few feet from a whale when 'blowing,' and, though purposely observing it, could never see that it ejected from its nostrils anything but the ordinary breath—a fact which might almost have been deduced from analogy. In the cold arctic air this breath is generally condensed, and falls upon those close at hand in the form of a dense spray which may have led seamen to suppose that this vapour was originally ejected in the form of water. Occasionally, when the whale blows just as it is rising out of or sinking in the sea, a little of the superincumbent water may be forced upwards by the column of breath. When the whale is wounded in the lungs, or in any of the blood-vessels immediately supplying them, blood, as might be expected, is ejected in the death-throes along with the breath. When the whaleman sees his prey 'spouting red,' he concludes that its end is not far distant; it is then mortally wounded."

Captain F. C. Hall, the commander of the unfortunate "Polaris" Expedition, thus describes, in his 'Life with the Esquimaux,' the spout of a whale:—"What this blowing is like," he says, "may be described by asking if the reader has ever seen the smoke produced by the firing of an old-fashioned flint-lock. If so, then he may understand the 'blow' of a whale—a flash in the pan and all is over."

Captain Scammon, an experienced American whaling captain, who, like Scoresby, could wield well both harpoon and pen, in his fine work on 'The Marine Mammals of the North-Western Coast of America,' writes to the same effect.

Mr. Herman Melville, who is not a naturalist, but has served before the mast in a sperm-whaler and borne his part in all the hardships and dangers of the chase, writes, in his remarkable book, 'The Whale':—'As for this 'whale-spout' you might almost stand in it, and yet be undecided as to what it is precisely. Nor is it at all prudent for the hunter to be over curious respecting it. For, even when coming into slight contact with the outer vapoury shreds of the jet, which will often happen, your skin will feverishly smart from the acrimony of the thing so touching you. And I know one who, coming into still closer contact with the spout—whether with some scientific object in view or otherwise I cannot say—the skin peeled off from his cheek and arm. Wherefore, among whalemen, the spout is deemed poisonous; they try to evade it. I have heard it said, and I do not much doubt it, that if the jet were fairly spouted into your eyes it would blind you."

The only other eye-witness I will cite is Mr. Bartlett, of the Zoological Gardens, whose experience and accuracy as an observer of the habits of animals is unsurpassed. He spent an autumn holiday in accompanying the late Mr. Frank Buckland and his colleagues, Messrs. Walpole and Young, in a tour of inquiry into the condition of the herring fishery in Scotland. When the commissioners left Peterhead, he remained there for a few days as the guest of Captain David Gray, of the steam whaler, "Eclipse," and as it was reported that large whales had been seen in the offing, his host invited him to go in search of them, and pay them a visit in his steam-launch. When about twelve miles out, they saw the whales, which were "finners," at a distance of four or five miles. Fourteen were counted—all large ones—some of which were seventy feet in length. On approaching them the captain shut off steam, and the launch was allowed to float in amongst them. So close were they to the boat that it would not have been difficult to jump upon the back of one of them had that been desirable. Mr. Bartlett tells me that he was greatly astonished by the immense force of the sudden outrush of air from their blow-holes, and the noise by which it was accompanied. He believes that the blast was strong enough to blow a man off the spiracle if he were seated on it. He authorizes me to say that having seen and watched these whales under such favourable circumstances, he entirely agrees with all that I have here written concerning the so-called "spout." The volume of hot, vaporous breath expelled is enormous, and this is accompanied by no small quantity of water, forced up by it when the blow-hole is opened below the surface.

An effect similar in appearance to the whale's spout is produced by the breathing of the hippopotamus. When this great beast opens its nostrils beneath the surface, water and spray are driven and scattered upward by the force of the air, but, of course, do not issue from the nasal passages. I have, also, seen this effect produced, though in a less degree, by the breathing of sea-lions.

I repeat, therefore, that not a drop of sea-water enters or passes out of the blow-hole of a whale. If the spiracle valve were in a condition to allow it to do so the animal would soon be drowned. Everyone knows the extreme irritation and the horrible feeling of suffocation caused to a human being, whilst eating or drinking, by a crumb or a little liquid "going the wrong way"—that is, being accidentally drawn to the air-passages instead of passing to the œsophagus. If water were to enter the bronchi of a whale it would instantly produce similar discomfort.

The neck of a popular error is hard to break; but it is time that one so palpable as that concerning the "spouting" of whales should cease to be promulgated and disseminated by fanciful illustrations of instructive books.

THE "SAILING" OF THE NAUTILUS.

ONE of the prettiest fables of the sea is that relating to the Paper Nautilus, the constructor and inhabitant of the delicate and beautiful shell which looks as if it were made of ivory no thicker than a sheet of writing paper.

FIG. 27.—THE PAPER NAUTILUS (*Argonauta argo*) SAILING.

It is an old belief that in calm weather it rises from the bottom of the sea, and, elevating its two broadly-expanded arms, spreads to the gentle air, as a sail, the membrane, light as a spider's web, by which they are united; and that, seated in its boat-like shell, it thus floats over the smooth surface of the ocean, steering and paddling with its other arms. Should storm arise or danger threaten, its masts and sail are lowered, its oars laid in, and the frail craft, filling with water, sinks gently beneath the waves.

When and where this picturesque idea originated I am unable to discover. It dates far back beyond the range of history; for Aristotle mentions it, and, unfortunately, sanctioned it. With the weight of his honoured name in its favour, this fallacy has maintained its place in popular belief, even to our own times; for the mantle of the great father of natural history, who was generally so marvellously correct, fell on none of his successors; Pliny, and Ælian, and the tribe of compilers who succeeded them, having been more concerned to make their histories sensational than to verify their statements.

Naturally, the Paper Nautilus has been the subject of many a poet's verses. Oppian wrote of it in his 'Halieutics':—

> "Sail-fish in secret, silent deeps reside,
> In shape and nature to the preke * allied;
> Close in their concave shells their bodies wrap,
> Avoid the waves and every storm escape.
> But not to mirksome depths alone confined;
> When pleasing calms have stilled the sighing wind,
> Curious to know what seas above contain,
> They leave the dark recesses of the main;
> Now, wanton, to the changing surface haste,
> View clearer skies, and the pure welkin taste.
> But slow they, cautious, rise, and, prudent, fear
> The upper region of the watery sphere;
> Backward they mount, and as the stream o'erflows,
> Their convex shells to pressing floods oppose.
> Conscious, they know that, should they forward move,
> O'erwhelming waves would sink them from above,

---

* The octopus.

> Fill the void space, and with the rushing weight,
> Force down th' inconstants to their former seat.
> When, first arrived, they feel the stronger blast,
> They lie supine and skim the liquid waste.
> The natural barks out-do all human art
> When skilful floaters play the sailor's part.
> Two feet they upward raise, and steady keep;
> These are the masts and rigging of the ship:
> A membrane stretch'd between supplies the sail,
> Bends from the masts, and swells before the gale.
> Two other feet hang paddling on each side,
> And serve for oars to row and helm to guide.
> 'Tis thus they sail, pleased with the wanton game,
> The fish, the sailor, and the ship, the same.
> But when the swimmers dread some dangers near
> The sportive pleasure yields to stronger fear.
> No more they, wanton, drive before the blasts,
> But strike the sails, and bring down all the masts;
> The rolling waves their sinking shells o'erflow,
> And dash them down again to sands below."

Montgomery also thus exquisitely paraphrases the same idea in his 'Pelican Island':—

> "Light as a flake of foam upon the wind,
> Keel upwards, from the deep emerged a shell,
> Shaped like the moon ere half her orb is filled.
> Fraught with young life, it righted as it rose,
> And moved at will along the yielding water.
> The native pilot of this little bark
> Put out a tier of oars on either side,
> Spread to the wafting breeze a twofold sail,
> And mounted up, and glided down, the billows
> In happy freedom, pleased to feel the air,
> And wander in the luxury of light."

Byron mentions the Nautilus in his 'Mutiny of the Bounty' as follows:—

> "The tender Nautilus, who steers his prow,
> The sea-born sailor of his shell canoe,
> The ocean Mab—the fairy of the sea,
> Seems far less fragile, and alas! more free.

He, when the lightning-winged tornadoes sweep
The surge, is safe: his port is in the deep;
And triumphs o'er the armadas of mankind
Which shake the world, yet crumble in the wind."

The very names by which this animal is known to the science which some persons erroneously think must be so hard and dry are poetic. In Aristotle's day it was called the *Nautilus* or *Nauticus*, "the mariner," and though two thousand two hundred years have passed since the great master wrote, the name still clings to it. As the Pearly Nautilus, a very different animal, also bears that name, Gualtieri perceived the necessity of distinguishing the Paper Nautilus from it, and was followed by Linnæus, who therefore entitled the genus to which the latter belongs, *Argonauta*, after the ship *Argo*, in which Jason and his companions sailed to Colchis to carry off the "Golden Fleece" suspended there in the temple of Mars, and guarded by brazen-hoofed bulls, whose nostrils breathed out fire and death, and by a watchful dragon that never slept. According to the Greek legend, the *Argo* was named after its builder Argus, the son of Danaus, and was the first ship that ever was built. Oppian ('Halieutics,' book I.) expresses his opinion that the Nautilus served as a model for the man who first conceived the idea of constructing a ship, and embarking on the waters :—

> "Ye Powers! when man first felled the stately trees,
> And passed to distant shores on wafting seas,
> Whether some god inspired the wondrous thought,
> Or chance found out, or careful study sought;
> If humble guess may probably divine,
> And trace th' improvement to the first design,
> Some wight of prying search, who wond'ring stood
> When softer gales had smoothed the dimpled flood,
> Observed these careless swimmers floating move,
> And how each blast the easy sailor drove;

> Hence took the hint, hence formed th' imperfect draught,
> And ship-like fish the future seaman taught.
> Then mortals tried the shelving hull to slope,
> To raise the mast, and twist the stronger rope,
> To fix the yards, let fly the crowded sails,
> Sweep through the curling waves, and court auspicious gales."

Pope, too, in his 'Essay on Man' (Ep. 3), adopted the idea in his exhortation—

> "Learn of the little Nautilus to sail,
> Spread the thin oar, and catch the driving gale."

Poetry, like the wizard's spell, can make

> "A nutshell seem a gilded barge,
> A sheeling seem a palace large,"

but the equally enchanting wand of science is able by a touch to dispel the illusion, and cause the object to appear in its true proportions. So with the fiction of the "Paper Sailor."

I have elsewhere described the affinities of the Nautili and their place in nature, therefore it will only be necessary for me here to allude to these very briefly, to explain the great and essential difference that exists between the two kinds of Nautilus which are popularly regarded as being one and the same animal.

The *Pearly* Nautilus (*Nautilus pompilius*) and the Argonaut, which from having a fragile shell of somewhat similar external form is called the *Paper* Nautilus, both belong to that great primary group of animals known as the *Mollusca*, and to the class of it called the *Cephalopoda*, from their having their head in the middle of that which is the foot in other mollusks. In the Cephalopoda the foot is split or divided into eight segments in some families, and in others into ten segments, which radiate from the central head, like so many rays. These rays are not only used as feet, but, being highly flexible, are adapted for employment also as prehensile arms, with which their owner captures its prey, and they are rendered more perfect for this purpose by being furnished with suckers which hold firmly to any surface to which they are applied. The Cephalopods which have the foot divided into ten of these segments or arms are called the *Decapoda*, those which have only eight of them are called the *Octopoda*. All of these have *two* plume-like gills—one on each side—and so are called *Dibranchiata*; and in the eight-armed section of these is the argonaut or Paper Nautilus. Of the Pearly Nautilus and the four-gilled order I shall have more to say by-and-by: at present we will follow the history of the argonaut.

Notwithstanding all that has been written of it, it is only within the last fifty years that this has been correctly understood. An eight-armed cuttle was recognised and named *Ocythoe*, which, instead of having, like the common octopus, all of its eight arms thong-like and tapering to a point, had the two dorsal limbs flattened into a broad thin membrane. Although this animal was sometimes seen dead without any covering, it was generally found contained in a thin and slightly elastic univalve shell of graceful form, and bearing some resemblance to an elegantly shaped boat. It did not penetrate to the bottom of this shell; it was not attached to it by any muscular ligament, nor was the shell moulded on its body, nor apparently made to fit it. Hence it was long regarded as doubtful, and even by naturalists so recent and eminent as Dumeril and De Blainville, whether

FIG. 28.—THE PAPER NAUTILUS (*Argonauta argo*) RETRACTED WITHIN ITS SHELL.

G

the octopod really secreted the shell, or whether, like the hermit-crab, it borrowed for its protection the shell of some other mollusk. Aristotle left the subject with the faithful acknowledgment: "As to the origin and growth of this shell nothing is yet exactly determined. It appears to be produced like other shells; but even this is not evident, any more than it is whether the animal can live without it." Pliny, as usual, instead of throwing light on the matter, obscured it. He regarded the shell as the property of a gasteropod like the snail, and the octopod as an amateur yachtsman who occasionally went on board and took a trip in the frail craft, and assisted its owner to navigate it for the fun of the thing. This is what he says about it*: "Mutianus reports that he saw in the Propontis a shell formed like a little ship, having the poop turned up and the prow pointed. An animal called the *Nauplius*, resembling an octopus, was enclosed in the shell with its owner, for its amusement in the following manner. When the sea is calm the guest lowers his arms, and uses them as oars and a helm, whilst the owner of the shell expands himself to catch the wind; so that one has the pleasure of carrying and sailing, and the other of steering. Thus, these two otherwise senseless animals take their pleasure together; but the meeting them sailing in their shell is a bad omen for mariners, and foretells some great calamity."

Although the animal was never found in any other shell, and the shell was never known to contain any other animal, and though, when the shell and the animal were found together they were always of proportionate size, this octopod, as I have said, was looked upon by some conchologists as a pirate who had taken possession of a ship which did not belong to him, until Madame Jeannette Power, a French lady then

* Naturalis Historia, lib. ix. cap. 30.

residing in Messina, having succeeded in keeping alive for a time an argonaut the shell of which had been broken in its capture, discovered that the animal quickly repaired the fracture, and reproduced the portions that had been broken off. Induced by this to make further experiments, she kept a number of living argonauts in cages sunk in the sea near the citadel of Messina, and in 1836 laid before the "Academy" at Catania the following results of her observations of them :—

1st. That the argonaut constructs the shell which it inhabits.

2nd. That it quits the egg entirely naked, and forms the shell after its birth.

3rd. That it can repair its shell, if necessary, by a fresh deposit of material having the same chemical composition as its original shell.

4th. That this material is secreted by the palmate, or sail, arms, and is laid on the outside of the shell, to the exterior of which these membranous arms are closely applied.

Madame Power was mistaken on two points. Firstly, the construction of the shell does not commence after the birth of the animal, but, as has been shown by M. Duvernoy, its rudimentary form is distinctly visible by the aid of the microscope in the embryo, whilst still in the egg; and secondly, she continued to believe in the use of the membranous arms as sails, and of the others as oars. This fallacy was exploded by Captain Sander Rang, an officer of the French navy, and "port-captain" at Algiers, who carefully followed up Madame Power's experiments, and confirmed the more important of them. Thus were set at rest questions which for centuries had divided the opinions of zoologists.

The "Paper Nautilus" is, in fact, a female octopod provided with a portable nest, in which to carry about and protect her eggs, instead of brooding over them in some cranny of a rock, or within the recesses of a pile of shells, as does her cousin the octopus. From the membranes of the two flattened and expanded arms she secretes and, if necessary, repairs her shell, and by applying them closely to its outer surface on each side, holds herself within it, for it is not fastened to her body by any attaching muscles. When disturbed or in danger she can loosen her hold, and, leaving her cradle, swim away independently of it. It has been said that, having once left it, she has not the ability nor perhaps the sagacity to re-enter her nest, and resume the guardianship of her eggs."[*] From my own observations of the breeding habits of other octopods I think this most improbable. The use and purpose of the shell of the argonaut will be better understood if I briefly describe what I have witnessed of the treatment of its eggs by its near relative, the octopus.

"The eggs of the octopus," as I have elsewhere said, "when first laid, are small, oval, translucent granules, resembling little grains of rice, not quite an eighth of an inch long. They grow along and around a common stalk, to which every egg is separately attached, as grapes form part of a bunch. Each of the elongated bunches is affixed by a glutinous secretion to the surface of a rock or stone (never to seaweed, as has been erroneously stated), and hangs pendent by its stalk in a long white cluster, like a magnified catkin of the filbert, or, to use Aristotle's simile, like the fruit of the white alder. The length and number of these bunches varies according to the size and condition of

---

[*] Appendix to Sir Edward Belcher's 'Voyage of the "Samarang,"' by Mr. Arthur Adams, assistant surgeon to the expedition.

the parent. Those produced by a small octopus are seldom more than about three inches long, and from twelve to twenty in number; but a full-grown female will deposit from forty to fifty of such clusters, each about five inches in length. I have counted the eggs of which these clusters are composed, and find that there are about a thousand in each : so that a large octopus produces in one laying, usually extended over three days, a progeny of from 40,000 to 50,000. I have seen an octopus, when undisturbed, pass one of her arms beneath the hanging bunches of her eggs, and, dilating the membrane on each side of it into a boat-shaped hollow, gather and receive them in it as in a trough or cradle which exhibited in its general shape and outline a remarkable similarity to the shell of the argonaut, with the eggs of which octopod its own are almost identical in form and appearance. Then she would caress and gently rub them, occasionally turning towards them the mouth of her flexible exhalent and locomotor tube, like the nozzle of a fireman's hose-pipe, so as to direct upon them a jet of the excurrent water. I believe that the object of this syringing process is to free the eggs from parasitic animalcules, and possibly to prevent the growth of conferva, which, I have found, rapidly overspreads those removed from her attention." *

It has been suggested that the syringing may be for the purpose of keeping the water surrounding the eggs well aerated; but this is evidently erroneous, for the water ejected from the tube has been previously deprived of its oxygen, and consequently of its health-giving properties, whilst passing over the gills of the parent. Week after week, for fifty days, a brooding octopus will continue to attend to her eggs with the most watchful and assiduous

* 'The Octopus,' 1873, p. 57.

care, seldom leaving them for an instant except to take food, which, without a brief abandonment of her position, would be beyond her reach. Aristotle asserted that while the female is incubating she takes no food. This is incorrect; but in every case of the kind that has come under my observation the mother octopod, whenever she has been obliged to leave her nest, has returned to it as quickly as possible; and so I believe can, and does, the female argonaut to her shell, and that, too, without any difficulty. In her case the numerous clusters of eggs are all united at their origin to one slender and tapering stalk

FIG. 29.—THE PAPER NAUTILUS (*Argonauta argo*) CRAWLING.

which is fixed by a spot of glutinous matter to the body-whorl of the spiral shell.

This "paper-sailor," then, whom the poets have regarded as endowed with so much grace and beauty, and living in luxurious ease, is but a fine lady octopus after all. Turn her out of her handsome residence, and, instead of the fairy skimmer of the seas, you have before you an object apparently as free from loveliness and romance as her sprawling, uncanny-looking, relative. Instead of floating in her pleasure boat over the surface of the sea, the argonaut ordinarily crawls along the bottom, carrying her shell above her, keel uppermost; and the broad extremities of the two arms are not hoisted as sails, nor allowed when at rest to dangle over the side of the "boat;" but are used as a kind of hood by which the animal retains the shell in its proper position, as a man bearing a load on his shoulders holds it with his hands. When she comes to the surface, or progresses by swimming instead of walking, she does so in the same manner as the octopus: namely, by the forcible expulsion of water from her funnel-like tube.

But if truth compels us to deprive her of the counterfeit halo conferred on her by poets, we can award her, on behalf of science, a far nobler crown; namely, that of the Queen of the whole great Invertebrate Animal Kingdom. For, the *Cephalopoda*, of which the argonaut is a highly

FIG. 30.—THE PAPER NAUTILUS (*Argonauta argo*) SWIMMING.

organised member, are not only the highest in their own division, the *Mollusca*, but they are as far superior to all other animals which have no backbones, as man stands lord and king over all created beings that possess them.

Although in outward shape the spiral shell of the Pearly Nautilus (*Nautilus pompilius*) somewhat resembles that of the argonaut, its internal structure is very different. A section of it shows that it is divided into several chambers, each of which is partitioned off from the adjoining ones, the last formed or external one, in which the animal lives, being much larger than the rest. The object and mode of construction of these chambers is as follows. As the animal grows, a constant secretion of new material takes place on the edge of the shell. By this unceasing process of the addition of new shell in the form of a circular curve or coil around the older portion, the whole rapidly increases in size, both in diameter, and in the length of the chamber. The Nautilus, requiring to keep the secreting portion of its mantle applied to the lip of the shell, finds the chamber in which it dwells gradually becoming inconveniently long for it, and therefore builds up a wall behind itself, and continues its work of enlarging its premises in front. Each of these walls, concave in front, towards the mouth of the shell, and

FIG. 31.—SHELL OF THE PAPER NAUTILUS (*Argonauta argo*).

concave behind, acts as a strong girder and support of the arch of the shell against the inward pressure of deep water : and it was formerly supposed that each successive chamber so constructed and vacated remained filled with air, and *thus* became an additional float by which the constantly increasing weight of the growing shell was counter-balanced. By this beautiful adjustment of augmented floating power to increased weight, the buoyancy of the shell would be secured and its specific gravity maintained as nearly as possible equal to that of the surrounding water. This adjustment does probably take place, but in a somewhat different manner. As the Nautilus inhabits a depth of from twenty to forty fathoms, it is evident that the air within its shell would be displaced by the pressure of such a column of water.* Accordingly, in every instance of the capture of a Nautilus the chambers of its shell have been found filled with water. It is not improbable that the fluid they contain may be less compressed, and exert less pressure from within outwards

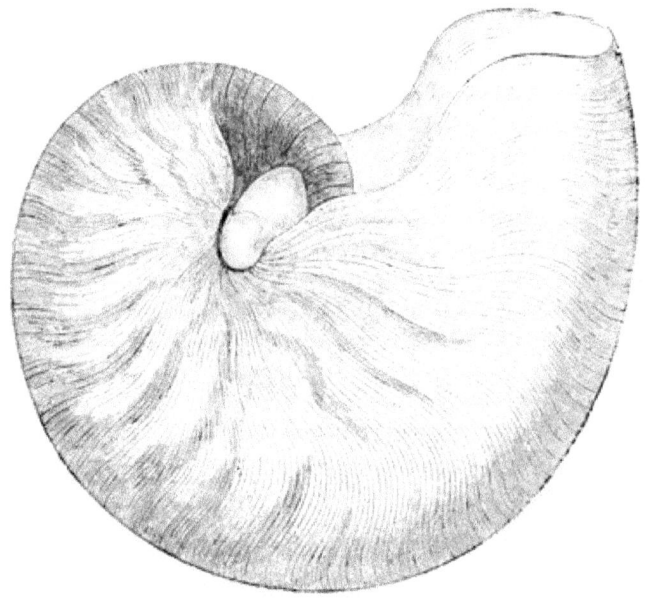

FIG. 32.—SHELL OF THE PEARLY NAUTILUS (*Nautilus pompilius*).

than that of the external superincumbent column of water, and that by this unbalanced pressure—under the same

---

* "At 100 fathoms the pressure exceeds 265 lbs. to the square inch. Empty bottles, securely corked, and sunk with weights beyond 100 fathoms, are always crushed. If filled with liquid the cork is driven in, and the liquid replaced by salt water ; and in drawing the bottle up again the cork is returned to the neck of the bottle, generally in a reversed position."—Sir F. Beaufort, quoted by Dr. S. P. Woodward in his 'Manual of the Mollusca.'

hydro-dynamic law which governs its mode of self-propulsion when swimming, and possibly in some degree within the control of the animal—the latter is relieved of much of the weight of its shell. When the Nautilus is at the bottom of the sea its movement is like that of a snail crawling along

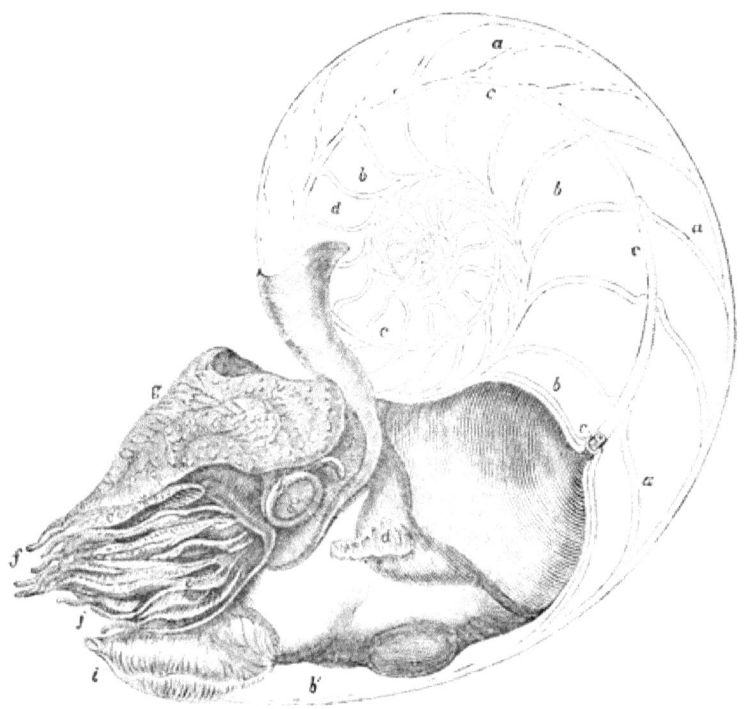

FIG. 33.—THE PEARLY NAUTILUS (*Nautilus pompilius*), AND SECTION OF ITS SHELL. *After Professor Owen.*

a a, Partitions; *b b*, chambers; *b'*, the last-formed chamber, in which the animal lives; *c c*, the siphuncle; *d*, attaching muscle; *e e*, the hollow arms; *f f*, retractile tentacles; *g*, muscular disk, or foot; *h*, the eye; *i*, position of funnel.

upon the ground with its shell above it. The shell, in proportion to the size of the animal that inhabits it, is a heavy one, and unless it were rendered semi-buoyant, its owner's strength would be severely taxed by the effort to drag it along. By the means indicated this portable domicile is borne lightly above the body of the Nautilus, without in any way impeding its progress.

The chambers are all connected by a membranous tube slightly coated with nacre, which is connected with a large sac in the body of the animal, near the heart, and passes through a circular orifice and a short projecting tube in the centre of each partition wall, till it ends in the smallest chamber at the inner extremity of the shell. Dean Buckland believed this "syphon" to be an hydraulic apparatus acting as a "fine adjustment" of the specific gravity of the shell, by admitting water within it when expanded, and excluding it when contracted. As it contains an artery and vein near its origin at the mantle, Professor Owen has regarded it as subservient to the maintenance of a low vitality in the vacated portion of the shell. Dr. Henry Woodward is of the opinion that, whilst in the early life of the Nautilus this siphuncle forms the main point of attachment between the animal and its shell, it is in the adult "simply an aborted embryonal organ whose function is now filled by the shell-muscles, but which in the more ancient and straight-shelled representatives of the group (the Orthoceratites) was not merely an embryonal but an important organ in the adult."

Every one knows the shell of the Pearly Nautilus. It may be purchased at any shell-shop in a seaside watering-place, and is imported by hundreds every year from Singapore.* It is abundant in the waters of the Indian Archipelago, especially about the Molucca and Philippine Islands, and on the shores of New Caledonia and the Fiji

* I need hardly say that before the nacreous layer of the shell from which this animal takes its name is made visible, an outer deposit of dense calcareous matter has to be removed by hydrochloric acid : the pearly surface thus exposed is then easily polished.

and Solomon Islands. It has also been found alive on Pemba Island, near Zanzibar. It seems strange, therefore, that until about half a century ago hardly anything was known of the animal that secretes and inhabits it. Rumphius, a Dutch naturalist, in his 'Rarities of Amboyna,' published, in 1705, a description of one with an engraving, incorrect in drawing, and deficient in detail; and until 1832 this was the only information which existed concerning it. The great Cuvier never saw one, and being acquainted only with the two-gilled cephalopods, he regarded the head-footed mollusks as absolutely isolated from all other animals in the kingdom of nature, even from the other classes of the mollusca. It seemed, however, to Professor Owen, then only nineteen years of age, that in the only living representative of the four-gilled order, *Nautilus pompilius*, might be found the "missing link." When, therefore, in the year 1824, his fellow-student, Mr. George Bennett, was about to sail from England to the Polynesian Islands, young Richard Owen earnestly charged his friend to do his utmost to obtain, and bring home in alcohol, a specimen of the much-coveted Pearly Nautilus. The opportunity did not occur till one warm and calm Monday evening, the 24th of August, 1829, when a living Nautilus was seen at the surface of the water not far distant from the ship, in Marekini Bay, on the south-west coast of the Island of Erromango, New Hebrides, in the South Pacific Ocean. It looked like a dead tortoise-shell cat, as the sailors said. As it began to sink as soon as it was observed, it was struck at with a boat-hook, and was thus so much injured that it died shortly after being taken on board the ship. The shell was destroyed, but the soft body of the animal was preserved in spirits, and great was the joy of Mr. Owen when, in July, 1831, Mr. Bennett arrived with it in England, and presented it to the Royal College of Surgeons. Mr. Owen was then Assistant-Conservator of the Museum of the College under Mr. Clift, who was afterwards his father-in-law. He immediately commenced to anatomise, describe, and figure his rare acquisition, and in the early part of 1832 published the result of his work in the form of a masterly treatise, which proved to be the foundation of his future fame.*

Mr. Owen's investigations confirmed his previous supposition that the Pearly Nautilus is inferior in its organisation to octopus, sepia, or any other known cephalopod; that it is not isolated, but that it recedes towards the gasteropods, to which belong the snail, the periwinkle, &c., and that in some of its characters its structure is analo-

* It is so interesting to most of us to know something of the early work of our greatest men, and of the tide in their affairs, which, taken at the flood, led on to fortune, that I hope I may be excused for referring to the period when the distinguished chief of the Natural History Department of the British Museum, the great comparative anatomist, the unrivalled palæontologist, the illustrious physiologist, the venerable and venerated friend of all earnest students, was beginning to attract the attention, and to receive the approbation of his seniors as a promising young worker. In Messrs. Griffith and Pidgeon's Supplement to Cuvier's 'Mollusca and Radiata,' published in 1834, the treatise in question is thus mentioned : "We have much pleasure in referring to a most excellent memoir on *Nautilus pompilius*, by Mr. Owen, with elaborate figures of the animal, its shell, and various parts, published by direction of the Council of the College of Surgeons. The reader will find the most satisfactory information on the subject, and the scientific public will earnestly hope that the present volume will be the first of a similar series." This hope has been more than fulfilled. Dean Buckland, in his 'Bridgewater Treatise,' wrote of this work : " I rejoice in the present opportunity of bearing testimony to the value of Professor Owen's highly philosophical and most admirable memoir—a work not less creditable to the author than honourable to the Royal College of Surgeons, under whose auspices the publication has been so handsomely conducted."

gously related to the still lower *annulosa*, or worms. Mr. Owen was just about to start for Paris with the intention of presenting a copy of his book to his celebrated contemporary and friend, and of showing him his dissections of the Nautilus which had been the subject of his research, when he heard of Baron Cuvier's death. It must have been to him a great sorrow and a grievous disappointment.

The Pearly Nautilus, then, is a true cephalopod, in that it has its foot divided and arranged in segments around its head, but the form and number of these segments are very different from those of any other of its class. Instead of there being eight, as in the argonaut and octopus, or ten, as in sepia and the calamaries, the Nautilus has about ninety projecting in every direction from around the mouth. They are short, round, and tapering, of about the length and thickness of the fingers of a child. Some of them are retractile into sheaths, and they are attached to fleshy processes (which might represent the child's hand), overlying each other, and covering the mouth on each side. They have none of the suckers with which the arms and tentacles of all the other cuttles are furnished, but their annulose structure, like the rings of an earthworm's body, gives them some little prehensile power. None of these numerous finger-like segments of the foot are flattened out like the broad membranous expansions of the argonaut, and, in fact, the Nautilus is without any members which can possibly be regarded as sails to hoist, or as oars with which to row. It has a strong beak, like the rest of the cuttles; but it has no ink-sac, for its shell is strong enough to afford it the protection which its two-gilled relatives have to seek in concealment.

The Pearly Nautilus usually creeps, like a snail, along the bed of the sea. It lives at the bottom, and feeds at the bottom, principally on crabs; and, as Dr. S. P. Woodward says, in his 'Manual of the Mollusca,' "perhaps often lies in wait for them, like some gigantic sea-anemone, with outspread tentacles." The shape of its shell is not well adapted for swimming, but it can ascend to the surface, if it so please, in the same manner as can all the cuttles— namely, by the outflow of water from its locomotor tube. The statement that it visits the surface of the sea of its own accord is at present, however, unconfirmed by observation.

But, if the Pearly Nautilus is the inferior and poor relation of the argonaut, it lives in a handsome house, and comes of an ancient lineage. The Ammonites, whose beautiful whorled and chambered shells, and the casts of them, are so abundant in every stratum, especially in the lias, the chalk, and the oolite, had four gills also. These Ammonites and the Nautili were amongst the earliest occupants of the ancient deep; and, with the Hamites, Turrilites, and others, lived upon our earth during a great portion of the incalculable period which has elapsed since it became fitted for animal existence, and in their time witnessed the rise and fall of many an animal dynasty. But they are gone now; and only the fossil relics of more than two thousand species (of which 188 were Nautili) remain to tell how important a race they were amongst the inhabitants of the old world seas. They and their congeners of the chambered shells, however, left one representative which has lived on through all the changes that have taken place on the surface of this globe since they became extinct—namely, *Nautilus pompilius*, the Nautilus of the pearly shell—the last of the Tetrabranchs.

I need offer no apology for endeavouring to explain the difference between the Nautilus of the chambered shell and the argonaut with the membranous arms which it was supposed to use as sails, when Webster, in his great standard dictionary, describes the one and figures the other as one and the same animal; and when a writer of the celebrity of Dr. Oliver Wendell Holmes also blends the two in the following poem, containing a sentiment as exquisite as its science is erroneous. I hope the latter distinguished and accomplished author, whose delightful writings I enjoy and highly appreciate, will pardon my criticism. I admit that the beauty of the thought might well atone for its inaccuracy, (of which the author is conscious,) were it not that the latter is made so attractive that truth appears harsh in disturbing it.

"THE CHAMBERED NAUTILUS."

"This is the ship of pearl, which poets feign
    Sails the unshadowed main,
    The venturous bark that flings
On the sweet summer wind its purpled wings,
In gulfs enchanted, where the siren sings,
    And coral reefs lie bare,
Where the cold sea-maids rise to sun their streaming hair.

Its webs of living gauze no more unfurl,
    Wrecked is the ship of pearl!
    And every chambered cell,
Where its dim, dreaming life was wont to dwell,
As the frail tenant shaped his growing shell,
    Before thee lies revealed,
Its irised ceiling rent, its sunless crypt unsealed!

Year after year beheld the silent toil
    That spread his lustrous coil;
    Still, as the spiral grew,
He left the past year's dwelling for the new,
Stole with soft step its shining archway through,
    Built up its idle door,
Stretched in his last-found home, and knew the old no more.

Thanks for the heavenly message brought by thee,
    Child of the wandering sea,
    Cast from her lap forlorn!
From the dead lips a clearer note is born
Than ever Triton blew from wreathèd horn!
    While on mine ear it rings,
Through the deep caves of thought I hear a voice that sings:—

' Build thee more stately mansions, O my soul,
    As the swift seasons roll!
    Leave thy low vaulted past;
Let each new temple, nobler than the last.
Shut thee from heaven with a dome more vast,
    Till thou at length art free,
Leaving thine outgrown shell by life's unresting sea.'"

BARNACLE GEESE—GOOSE BARNACLES.

THE belief that some wild geese, instead of being hatched from eggs, like other birds, grew on trees and rotten wood has never been surpassed as a specimen of ignorant credulity and persistent error.

There are two principal versions of this absurd notion. One is that certain trees, resembling willows, and growing always close to the sea, produced at the ends of their branches fruit in form like apples, and each containing the embryo of a goose, which, when the fruit was ripe, fell into the water and flew away. The other is that the geese were bred from a fungus growing on rotten timber floating at sea, and were first developed in the form of worms in the substance of the wood.

When and whence this improbable theory had its origin is uncertain. Aristotle does not mention it, and consequently Pliny and Ælian were deprived of the pleasure they would have felt in handing down to posterity, without investigation or correction, a statement so surprising. It is, comparatively, a modern myth; although we find that it was firmly established in the middle of the twelfth century, for Gerald de Barri, known in literature as Giraldus Cambrensis, mentions it in his 'Topographia Hiberniæ,' published in 1187. Giraldus, who was Archdeacon of Brecknock in the reign of Henry II., and tried hard, more than once, for the bishopric of St. David's, the functions of which he had temporarily administered without obtaining the title, was a vigorous and zealous reformer of Church abuses. Amongst the laxities of discipline against which he found it necessary to protest was the custom then prevailing of eating these Barnacle geese during Lent, under the plea that their flesh was not that of birds, but of fishes. He writes:—

"There are here many birds which are called Bernacae, which nature produces in a manner contrary to nature, and very wonderful. They are like marsh-geese but smaller. They are produced from fir-timber tossed about at sea, and are at first like geese upon it. Afterwards they hang down by their beaks, as if from a sea-weed attached to the wood, and are enclosed in shells that they may grow the more freely. Having thus, in course of time, been clothed with a strong covering of feathers, they either fall into the water, or seek their liberty in the air by flight. The embryo geese derive their growth and nutriment from the moisture of the wood or of the sea, in a secret and most marvellous manner. I have seen with my own eyes more than a thousand minute bodies of these birds hanging from one piece of timber on the shore, enclosed in shells and already formed. Their eggs are not impregnated *in coitu*, like those of other birds, nor does the bird sit upon its eggs to hatch them, and in no corner of the world have they been known to build a nest. Hence the bishops and clergy in some parts of Ireland are in the habit of partaking of these birds on fast days, without scruple. But in doing so they are led into sin. For, if any one were to eat of the leg of our first parent, although he (Adam) was not born of flesh, that person could not be adjudged innocent of eating flesh."

This fable of the geese appears, however, to have been current at least a hundred years before Giraldus wrote, for Professor Max Müller, who treats of it in one of his "Lectures on the Science of Language," amongst many interesting references there given, quotes a Cardinal of the eleventh century, Petrus Damianus, who clearly describes, that version of it which represents the birds as bursting, when fully fledged, from fruit resembling apples.

It is a curious fact that these Barnacle geese have

troubled the priesthood of more than one creed as to the instructions they should give to the laity concerning the use of them as food. The Jews—all those, at least, who maintain a strict observance of the Hebrew Law—eat no meat but that of animals which have been slaughtered in a certain prescribed manner; and a doubt arose amongst them at the period we refer to, whether these geese should be killed as flesh or as fish. Professor Max Müller cites Mordechai,* as asking whether these birds are fruits, fish, or flesh; that is, whether they must be killed in the Jewish way, as if they were flesh. Mordechai describes them as birds which grow on trees, and says, "the Rabbi Jehuda, of Worms (who died 1216) used to say that he had heard from his father, Rabbi Samuel, of Speyer (about 1150), that Rabbi Jacob Tham, of Ramerü (who died 1171), the grandson of the great Rabbi Rashi (about 1140), had decided that they must be killed as flesh."

Pope Innocent III. took the same view; for at the Lateran Council, in 1215, he prohibited the eating of Barnacle geese during Lent. In 1277, Rabbi Izaak, of Corbeil, determined to be on the safe side, forbade altogether the eating of these birds by the Jews, "because they were neither flesh nor fish."

Michael Bernhard Valentine,† quoting Wormius, says that this question caused much perplexity and disputation amongst the doctors of the Sorbonne; but that they passed an ordinance that these geese should be classed as fishes, and not as birds; and he adds, that in consequence of this decision large numbers of these birds were annually sent to Paris from England and Scotland, for consumption in

---

* Riva, 1559, leaf 142ª.
† 'Historia Simplicium,' lib. iii. p. 327.

Lent. Sir Robert Sibbald * refers to this, and says that Normandy was the locality from which the French capital was reported to be principally supplied; but that in fact the greater number of these geese came from Holland. The date of this edict is not given.

Professor Max Müller says that in Brittany, Barnacle geese are still allowed to be eaten on Fridays, and that the Roman Catholic Bishop of Ferns may give permission to people out of his diocese to eat these birds at his table.

In Bombay, also, where fish is prohibited as food to some classes of the population, the priests call this goose a "sea-vegetable," under which name it is allowed to be eaten.

Various localities were mentioned as the breeding-places of these arboreal geese. Gervasius of Tilbury,† writing about 1211, describes the process of their generation in full detail, and says that great numbers of them grew in his time upon the young willow trees which abounded in the neighbourhood of the Abbey of Faversham, in the county of Kent, and within the Archiepiscopate of Canterbury. The bird was there commonly called the *Barneta*.

Hector Boethius, or Boece, the old Scottish historian, combats this version of the story. His work, written in Latin, in 1527, was translated into quaint Scottish in 1540, by John Bellenden, Archdeacon of Murray. In his fourteenth chapter, "Of the nature of claik geis, and of the syndry maner of thair procreatioun, And of the ile of Thule," he says:—

"Restis now to speik of the geis generit of the see namit clakis. Sum men belevis that thir clakis growis on treis be the nebbis. Bot thair opinioun is vane. And becaus the nature and procreatioun of thir clakis is strange we have maid na lytyll laubore and deligence to

---

* Prodrom. Hist. Nat. Scot. parts 2, lib. iii. p. 21, 1684.
† Otia Imperialia, iii. 123.

serche ye treuth and verite yairof, we have salit throw ye seis quhare thir clakis ar bred, and I fynd be gret experience, that the nature of the seis is mair relevant caus of thir procreatioun than ony uther thyng."

From the circumstances attending the finding of "ane gret tree that was brocht be alluvion and flux of the see to land, in secht of money pepyll besyde the castell of Petslego, in the yeir of God ane thousand iiii. hundred lxxxx, and of a see tangle hyngand full of mussill schellis," brought to him by "Maister Alexander Galloway, person of Kynkell," who knowing him to be "richt desirus of sic uncouth thingis came haistely with the said tangle," he arrives at the conclusion, by a process of reasoning highly satisfactory and convincing to himself, that,

"Be thir and mony othir resorcis and examplis we can not beleif that thir clakis ar producit be ony nature of treis or rutis thairof, but allanerly be the nature of the Oceane see, quhilk is the caus and production of mony wonderful thingis. And becaus the rude and ignorant pepyl saw oftymes the fruitis that fel of the treis (quhilkis stude neir the see) convertit within schort tyme in geis, thai belevit that thir geis grew apon the treis hingand be thair nebbis sic lik as appillis and uthir frutis hingis be thair stalkis, bot thair opinioun is nocht to be sustenit. For als sone as thir appillis or frutis fallis of the tre in the see flude thay grow first wormeetin. And be schort process of tyme are alterat in geis."

In describing the bird thus produced, Boethius declares that the male has a sharp, pointed beak, like the gallinaceous birds, but that in the female the beak is obtuse as in other geese and ducks.

According to other authors, this wonderful production of birds from living or dead timber was not confined to England and Scotland. Vincentius Bellovacensis [*] (1190-

---

[*] For this quotation and the following one I am indebted to Professor Max Müller's Lecture before referred to.

1264) in his 'Speculum Naturæ,' xvii. 40, states that it took place in Germany, and Jacob de Vitriaco (who died 1244) mentions its occurrence in certain parts of Flanders.

Jonas Ramus gives a somewhat different version of the process as it occurs in Norway. He writes : * "It is said that a particular sort of geese is found in Nordland, which leave their seed on old trees, and stumps and blocks lying in the sea ; and that from that seed there grows a shell fast to the trees, from which shell, as from an egg, by the heat of the sun, young geese are hatched, and afterwards grow up ; which gave rise to the fable that geese grow upon trees."

But, strange to say, if any painstaking enquirer, wishing to investigate the matter for himself, went to a locality where it was said the phenomenon regularly occurred, he was sure to find that he had literally, "started on a wild-goose chase," and had come to the wrong place. This was the experience of Æneas Sylvius Piccolomini, afterwards Pope Pius II., who complained that miracles will always flee farther and farther away ; for when he was on a visit (about 1430) to King James I., of Scotland,† and enquired after the tree which he most eagerly desired to see, he was told that it grew much farther north, in the Orkney Islands.

Notwithstanding the suspicious fact that the prodigy receded like Will o' the Wisp, whenever it was persistently followed up, Sebastian Munster, who relates ‡ the foregoing

* 'Chorographical Description of Norway,' p. 244.

† Æneas Sylvius gives us information concerning the personal appearance of his royal host, whom he describes as, " *hominem quadratum et multa pinguedine gravem*,"—literally, " a square-built man, heavy with much fat."

‡ 'Cosmographia Universalis,' p. 49, 1572.

anecdote of Æneas Sylvius, appears to have entertained no doubt of the truth of the report, for he writes :—

FIG. 34.—THE GOOSE TREE. *Copied from Gerard's 'Herball,' 1st edition.**

" In Scotland there are trees which produce fruit, conglomerated of

---

* The original of this picture is a small wood-cut in Matthias de Lobel's 'Stirpium Historia,' published in 1870. The birds within the shells were added by Gerard. Aldrovandus, in copying it, gave leaves to the tree, as shown on page 110.

their leaves; and this fruit, when in due time it falls into the water beneath it, is endowed with new life, and is converted into a living bird, which they call the 'tree-goose.' This tree grows in the Island of Pomonia, which is not far from Scotland, towards the north. Several old cosmographers, especially Saxo Grammaticus, mention the tree, and it must not be regarded as fictitious, as some new writers suppose."

Julius Cæsar Scaliger* (1540) gives another reading of the legend, in which it is asserted that the leaves which fall from the tree into the water are converted into fishes, and those which fall upon the land become birds.

Thus this extraordinary belief held sway, and remained strong and invincible, although from time to time some man of sense and independent thought attempted to turn the tide of popular error. Albertus Magnus (who died 1280) showed its absurdity, and declared that he had seen the bird referred to lay its eggs and hatch them in the ordinary way. Roger Bacon (who died in 1294) also contradicted it, and Belon, in 1551, treated it with ridicule and contempt. Olaus Wormius † seems to have believed in it, though he wrote cautiously about it. Olaus Magnus (1553) mentions it, and apparently accepts it as a fact, occurring in the Orkneys, on the authority of "a Scotch historian who diligently sets down the secrets of things," and then dismisses it in three lines.

Passing over many other writers on the subject, we come to the time of the reign of Queen Elizabeth, when (in 1597) "John Gerarde, Master in Chirurgerie, London," published his "Herball, or Generall Historie of Plants gathered by him," and in the last chapter thereof solemnly declared, that he had actually witnessed the transformation of "certaine shell fish" into Barnacle Geese, as follows.

* Exercit. 59, sect. 2.   † 'Museum,' p. 257.

Of the Goose tree, Barnacle tree, or the tree bearing Geese.

Britanica Conchæ anatiferæ.

THE BREED OF BARNACLES.

¶ *The Description.*

Hauing trauelled from the Grasses growing in the bottome of the fenny waters, the Woods, and mountaines, euen vnto Libanus itselfe ; and also the sea, and bowels of the same, wee are arriued at the end of our History ; thinking it not impertinent to the conclusion of the same, to end with one of the maruels of this land (we may say of the World). The history whereof to set forth according to the worthinesse and raritie thereof, would not only require a large and peculiar volume, but also a deeper search into the bowels of Nature, then my intended purpose will suffer me to wade into, my sufficiencie also considered ; leauing the History thereof rough hewen, vnto some excellent man, learned in the secrets of nature, to be both fined and refined ; in the meane space take it as it falleth out, the naked and bare truth, though vnpolished. There are found in the North parts of Scotland and the Islands adiacent, called Orchades, certaine trees whereon do grow certaine shells of a white colour tending to russet, wherein are contained little liuing creatures : which shells in time of maturity doe open, and out of them grow those little liuing things, which falling into the water do become fowles, which we call Barnacles ; in the North of England, brant Geese ; and in Lancashire, tree Geese : but the other that do fall vpon the land perish and come to nothing. Thus much by the writings of others, and also from the mouthes of people of those parts, which may very well accord with truth.

But what our eies haue seene, and hands haue touched we shall declare. There is a small Island in Lancashire, called the Pile of Foulders, wherein are found the broken pieces of old and bruised ships some whereof haue beene cast thither by shipwracke, and also the trunks and bodies with the branches of old and rotten trees, cast vp there likewise ; whereon is found a certaine spume or froth that in time breedeth vnto certaine shells, in shape like those of the Muskle, but sharper pointed, and of a whitish colour ; wherein is contained a thing in forme like a lace of silke finely wouen as it were together, of a whitish colour, one end whereof is fastened vnto the inside of the shell, euen as the fish of Oisters and Muskles are : the other end is made fast vnto the belly of a rude masse or lumpe, which in time commeth to the shape and forme of a Bird : when it is perfectly formed the shell gapeth open, and the first thing that appeareth is the foresaid lace or string ; next come the legs of the bird hanging out, and as it groweth greater it openeth the shell by degrees, til at length it is all come forth, and hangeth onely by the bill : in short space after it commeth to full maturitie, and falleth into the sea, where it gathereth feathers, and groweth to a fowle bigger than a Mallard, and lesser than a Goose, hauing blacke legs and bill or beake, and feathers blacke and white, spotted in such manner as is our Magpie, called in some places a Pie-Annet, which the people of Lancashire call by no other name than a tree Goose : which place aforesaid, and all those parts adjoyning do so much abound therewith, that one of the best is bought for three pence. For the truth hereof, if any doubt, may it please them to repaire vnto me, and I shall satisfie them by the testimonie of good witnesses.

Moreover, it should seeme that there is another sort hereof; the History of which is true, and of mine owne knowledge ; for trauelling vpon the shore of our English coast betweene Douer and Rumney, I found the trunke of an old rotten tree, which (with some helpe that I procured by Fishermen's wiues that were there attending their husbands' returne from the sea) we drew out of the water vpon dry land ; vpon this rotten tree I found growing many thousands of long crimson bladders, in shape like vnto puddings newly filled, before they be sodden, which were very cleere and shining ; at the nether end whereof did grow a shell fish, fashioned somewhat like a small Muskle, but much whiter, resembling a shell fish that groweth vpon the rockes about Garnsey and Garsey, called a Lympit : many of these shells I brought with me to London, which after I had opened I found in them liuing things without forme or shape ; in others which were neerer come to ripenesse I found liuing things that were very naked, in shape like a Bird : in others, the Birds couered with soft downe, the shell halfe open, and the Bird ready to fall out, which no doubt were the Fowles called Barnacles. I dare not absolutely auouch euery circumstance of the first part of this history, concerning the tree that beareth those buds aforesaid, but will leaue it to a further consideration ; howbeit, that which I haue seene with mine eies, and handled with mine

hands, I dare confidently auouch, and boldly put downe for verity.
Now if any will object that this tree which I saw might be one of those
before mentioned, which either by the waues of the sea or some violent
wind had beene ouerturned as many other trees are; or that any trees
falling into those seas about the Orchades, will of themselues bear
the like Fowles, by reason of those seas and waters, these being so
probable conjectures, and likely to be true, I may not without prejudice
gainsay, or endeauour to confute.

¶ *The Place.*

The bordes and rotten plankes whereon are found these shels breeding the Barnakle, are taken vp in a small Island adioyning to Lancashire, halfe a mile from the main land, called the Pile of Foulders.

¶ *The Time.*

They spawn as it were in March and Aprill; the Geese are formed in May and June, and come to fulnesse of feathers in the moneth after.

And thus hauing through God's assistance discoursed somewhat at large of Grasses, Herbes, Shrubs, Trees, and Mosses, and certaine Excrescenses of the Earth, with other things moe, incident to the historie thereof, we conclude and end our present Volume, with this wonder of England. For the which God's name be euer honored and praised.

Gerard was probably a good botanist and herbalist; but Thomas Johnson, the editor of a subsequent issue of his book, tells us that

"He, out of a propense good will to the publique advancement of this knowledge, endeavoured to performe therein more than he could well accomplish, which was partly through want of sufficient learning; but," he adds, "let none blame him for these defects, seeing he was neither wanting in pains nor good will to performe what hee intended: and there are none so simple but know that heavie burthens are with most paines vndergone by the weakest men; and although there are many faults in the worke, yet iudge well of the Author; for, as a late writer well saith :—'To err and to be deceived is human, and he must seek solitude who wishes to live only with the perfect.'"

It is difficult to comply with the request to think well of one who, writing as an authority, deliberately promulgated, with an affectation of piety, that which he must have known to be untrue, and who was, moreover, a shameless plagiarist; for Gerard's ponderous book is little more than a translation of Dodonæus, whole chapters having been taken verbatim from that comparatively unread author without acknowledgment.

After this series of erroneous observations, self-delusion, and ignorant credulity, it is refreshing to turn to the pages of the two little thick quarto volumes of Gaspar Schott.* This learned Jesuit made himself acquainted with everything that had been written on the subject, and besides the authors I have referred to, quotes and compares the statements of Majolus, Abrahamus Ortelius, Hieronymus Cardanus, Eusebius, Nierembergius, Deusingius, Odoricus, Gerhardus de Vera, Ferdinand of Cordova, and many others. He then gives, firmly and clearly, his own opinion that the assertion that birds in Britain spring from the fruit or leaves of trees, or from wood, or from fungus, or from shells, is without foundation, and that neither reason, experience, nor authority tend to confirm it. He concedes that worms may be bred in rotting timber, and even that they may be of a kind that fly away on arriving at maturity (referring probably to caterpillars being developed into moths), but that birds should be thus generated, he says, is simply the repetition of a vulgar error, for not one of the authors whom he has examined has seen what they all affirm; nor are they able to bring forward a single eye-witness of it. He asks how it can be possible that animals so large and so highly-organised as these birds

* 'Physica Curiosa, sive Mirabilia Naturæ et Artis,' 1662, lib. ix. cap. xxii. p. 960.

can grow from puny animalcules generated in putrid wood. He further declares that these British geese are hatched from eggs like other geese, which he considers proved by the testimony of Albertus Magnus, Gerhardus de Vera, and of Dutch seamen, who, in 1569, gave their written declaration that they had personally seen these birds sitting on their eggs, and hatching them, on the coasts of Nova Zembla.

FIG. 35.—THE BARNACLE GOOSE TREE.   *After Aldrovandus.*

In marked and disgraceful contrast with this careful and philosophical investigation and its author's just deductions from it, is 'A Relation concerning Barnacles by Sir Robert Moray, lately one of His Majesty's Council for the Kingdom of Scotland,' read before the Royal Society, and published in the 'Philosophical Transactions,' No. 137, January and February, 1677-8.

Describing "a cut of a large Firr-tree of about two and a half feet diameter, and nine or ten feet long," which he saw on the shore in the Western Islands of Scotland, and which had become so dry that many of the Barnacle shells with which it had been covered had been rubbed off, he says:—

"Only on the parts that lay next the ground there still hung multitudes of little Shells, having within them little Birds, perfectly

FIG. 36.—DEVELOPMENT OF BARNACLES INTO GEESE. *After Aldrovandus.*

shap'd, supposed to be Barnacles. The Shells hung very thick and close one by another, and were of different sizes. Of the colour and consistence of Muscle-Shells, and the sides and joynts of them joyned with such a kind of film as Muscle-Shells are, which serves them for a Hing to move upon, when they open and shut. . . . The Shells hang at the Tree by a Neck longer than the Shell, of a kind of Filmy substance, round, and hollow, and creased, not unlike the Wind-pipe of a chicken, spreading out broadest where it is fastened to the Tree, from which it seems to draw and convey the matter which serves for the growth and vegetation of the Shell and the little Bird within it. This Bird in every Shell that I opened, as well the least as the biggest, I found so curiously and compleatly formed, that there appeared nothing wanting as to internal parts, for making up a perfect Sea-fowl: every little part appearing so distinctly that the whole looked like a large Bird seen through a concave or diminishing glass, colour and feature being everywhere so clear and neat. The little Bill, like that of a Goose; the eyes marked; the Head, Neck, Breast, Wings, Tail, and Feet formed, the Feathers everywhere perfectly shap'd, and blackish coloured; and the Feet like those of other Water-fowl, to my best remembrance. All being dead and dry, I did not look after the internal parts of them. Nor did I ever see any of the little Birds alive, nor met with anybody that did. Only some credible persons have assured me they have seen some as big as their fist."

It seems almost incredible that little more than two hundred years ago this twaddle should not only have been laid before the highest representatives of science in the land, but that it should have been printed in their "Transactions" for the further delusion of posterity.

Ray, in his edition of Willughby's Ornithology, published in the same year as the above, contradicted the fallacy as strongly as Gaspar Schott; and (except that he incidentally admits the possibility of spontaneous generation in some of the lower animals, as insects and frogs) in language so similar that I think he must have had Schott's work before him when he wrote.

Aldrovandus * tells us that an Irish priest, named Octavianus, assured him with an oath on the Gospels that he had seen and handled the geese in their embryo condition; and he adds that he "would rather err with the majority than seem to pass censure on so many eminent writers who have believed the story."

In 1629 Count Maier (Michaelus Meyerus—these old authors when writing in Latin, latinized their names also)

* 'Ornithologia,' lib. xix. p. 173, ed. 1603.

published a monograph 'On the Tree-bird'* in which he explains the process of its birth, and states that he opened a hundred of the goose-bearing shells and found the rudiments of the bird fully formed.

> So slow Bootes underneath him sees,
> In th' icy isles, those goslings hatched on trees,
> Whose fruitful leaves, falling into the water,
> Are turned, they say, to living fowls soon after;
> So rotten sides of broken ships do change,
> To barnacles, O, transformation strange!
> 'Twas first a green tree; then a gallant hull;
> Lately a mushroom; then a flying gull.†

Now, let us turn from fiction to facts.

Almost every one is acquainted with at least one kind of the Barnacle shells which were supposed to enclose the

FIG. 37.—SECTION OF A SESSILE BARNACLE. *Balanus tintinnabulum.*

embryo of a goose, namely the small white conical hillocks which are found, in tens of thousands, adhering to stones, rocks, and old timber such as the piles of piers, and may be seen affixed to the shells of oysters and mussels in any fishmonger's shop. The little animals which secrete and

* 'De Volucri Arborea,' 1629.
† Du Bartas' "Divine Week" p. 228. Joshua Sylvester's translation.

inhabit these shells belong to a sub-class and order of the Crustacea, called the *Cirrhopoda*, because their feet (*poda*), which in the crab and lobster terminate in claws, are modified into tufts of curled hairs (*cirri*), or feathers. When the animal is alive and active under water, a crater may be seen to open on the summit of the little shelly mountain, and, as if from the mouth of a miniature volcano, there issue from this aperture, from between two inner shells, the *cirri* in the form of a feathery hand, which clutches at the water within its reach, and is then quickly retracted within the shell. During this movement the hair-fringed fingers have filtered from the water and conveyed towards the mouth within the shell, for their owner's nutriment, some minute solid particles or animalcules, and this action of the casting-net alternately shot forth and retracted continues for hours incessantly, as the water flows over its resting-place. The animal can live for a long time out of water, and in some situations thus passes half its life. Under such circumstances, the shells, containing a reserve of moisture, remain firmly closed until the return of the tide brings a fresh supply of water and food. These are the "acorn-barnacles," the *balani*, commonly known in some localities as "chitters."

Barnacles of another kind are those furnished with a long stem, or peduncle, which Sir Robert Moray described as "round, hollow, and creased, and not unlike the wind-pipe of a chicken." The stem has, in fact, the ringed formation of the annelids, or worms. The shelly valves are thin, flat, and in shape somewhat like a mitre. They are composed of five pieces, two on each side, and one, a kind of rounded keel along the back of the valves, by which these are united. The shells are delicately tinted with lavender or pale blue varied with white, and the edges are frequently of a bright chrome yellow or orange colour.

It is not an uncommon occurrence for a large plank entirely covered with these "necked barnacles" to be found floating at sea and brought ashore for exhibition at some watering-place; and I have more than once sent portions of such planks to the Aquaria at Brighton, and the Crystal Palace.

It is most interesting to watch a dense mass of living cirripedes so closely packed together that not a speck of

FIG. 38.—PEDUNCULATED BARNACLES. (*Lepas anatifera*.)

the surface of the wood is left uncovered by them; their fleshy stalks overhanging each other, and often attached in clusters to those of some larger individuals; their plumose casting-nets ever gathering in the food that comes within their reach, and carrying towards the mouth any solid particles suitable for their sustenance. How much of insoluble matter barnacles will eliminate from the water is shown by the rapidity with which they will render turbid sea water clear and transparent. The most common species of these "necked barnacles" bears the name of "*Lepas anatifera*," "the duck-bearing *Lepas*." It was so entitled by Linnæus, in recognition of its having been connected with the fable, which, of course, met with no credit from him.

Fig. 39 represents the figure-head of a ship, partly covered with barnacles, which was picked up about thirty miles off Lowestoft on the 22nd of October, 1857. It was described in the *Illustrated London News*, and the pro-

FIG. 39.—A SHIP'S FIGURE-HEAD WITH BARNACLES ATTACHED TO IT.

prietors of that paper have kindly given me a copy of the block from which its portrait was printed.

Others of the barnacles affix themselves to the bottoms of ships, or parasitically upon whales and sharks, and those of the latter kind often burrow deeply into the skin of their host. Fig. 40 is a portrait of a *Coronula diadema* taken from the nose of a whale stranded at Kintradwell, in the north of Scotland, in 1866, and sent to the late Mr. Frank Buckland. Growing on this *Coronula* are three of the curious eared barnacles, *Conchoderma aurita*, the *Lepas aurita* of Linnæus. The species of the whale from which these Barnacles were taken was not mentioned, but it was probably the "hunch-backed" whale, *Megaptera longimana*,

FIG. 40.—WHALE BARNACLE (*Coronula diadema*), WITH THREE *Conchoderma aurita* ATTACHED TO IT.

which is generally infested with this *Coronula*. This very illustrative specimen was, and I hope still is, in Mr. Buckland's Museum at South Kensington. It was described by him in *Land and Water*, of May 19th, 1866, and I am indebted to the proprietors of that paper for the accompanying portrait of it.

The young Barnacle when just extruded from the shell of its parent is a very different being from that which it will be in its mature condition. It begins its life in a form exactly like that of an entomostracous crustacean, and, like a Cyclops, has one large eye in the middle of its forehead. In this state it swims freely, and with great activity. It undergoes three moults, each time altering its figure, until at the third exuviation it has become enclosed in a

FIG. 41.—A YOUNG BARNACLE. (*Larva of Chthamalus stellatus.*)

bivalve shell, and has acquired a second eye. It is now ready to attach itself to its abiding-place; so, selecting its future residence, it presses itself against the wood, or whatever the substance may be, pours out from its two antennæ a glutinous cement, which hardens in water, and thus fastens itself by the front of its head, is henceforth a fixture for life, and assumes the adult form in which most persons know it best.[*]

[*] If any of my readers wish to observe the development of young barnacles they may easily do so. The method I have generally adopted has been as follows: Procure a shallow glass or earthenware milk-pan that will hold at least a gallon. Fill this to within an inch

It is unnecessary for me to describe more minutely the anatomy of the Cirripedes; I have said enough to show

---

of the top with sea-water, and place it in any shaded part of a room—not in front of a window. Put in the pan six or eight pebbles or clean shells of equal height, say 1½ or 2 inches, and on them lay a clean sheet of glass, which, by resting on the pebbles, is brought to within about 2½ inches of the surface of the water. Select some limpets or mussels having acorn-barnacles on them; carefully cut out the limpet or mussel, and clean nicely the interior of the shell; then place a dozen or more of these shells on the sheet of glass, and the barnacles upon them will be within convenient reach of any observation with a magnifying glass. If this be done in the month of March, the experimenter will not have to wait long before he sees young *Balani* ejected from the summits of some of the shells. Up to the moment of their birth each of them is inclosed in a little cocoon or case, in shape like a canary-seed, and most of them are tossed into the world whilst still enclosed in this. In a few seconds this casing is ruptured longitudinally, apparently by the struggles of its inmate, which escapes at one end, like a butterfly emerging from its chrysalis, and swims freely to the surface of the water, leaving the split cocoon or case at the bottom of the pan. Some few of the young barnacles seem to be freed from the cocoon before, or at the moment of, extrusion. From three to a dozen or more of these escape with each protrusion of the cirri of the parent, and as the parturient barnacle will put forth its feathery casting net at least twenty times in a minute for an hour or more, it follows that as many as ten thousand young ones may be produced in an hour. These, as they are cast forth at each pulsation of the parent's cirri, fall upon the clean sheet of glass, and may be taken up in a pipette, and placed under a microscope, or removed to a smaller vessel of sea-water, for minute and separate investigation. It seems strange that animals which, like the oyster and the barnacles, are condemned in their mature condition to lead so sedentary a life, should in the earlier stages of their existence swim freely and merrily through the water—young fellows seeking a home, and when they have found it, although their connubial life must be a very tame one, settling down, and not caring to rove about any more for the remainder of their days. These young *Balani* dart about like so many water-fleas, and yet, after a few days of freedom, they become fixed and immovable, the inhabitants of the pyramidal shells which grow in such abundance on other shells, stones, and old wood.

the nature of the plumose appurtenances which, hanging from the dead shells, were supposed to be the feathers of a little bird within ; but it is difficult to understand how any one could have seen in the natural occupant of the shell, "the little bill, like that of a goose, the eyes, head, neck, breast, wings, tail, and feet, like those of other water-fowl," so precisely and categorically detailed by Sir Robert Moray. As Pontoppidan, who denounced the whole story, as being "without the least foundation," very truly says, "One must take the force of imagination to help to make it look so !"

As to the origin of the myth, I venture to differ entirely from philologists who attribute it to "language," and "a similarity of names," for, although, as Professor Max Müller observes in one of his lectures, "words without definite meanings are at the bottom of nearly all our philosophical and religious controversies," it certainly is not applicable in this instance. Every quotation here given shows that the mistake arose from the supposed resemblance of the plumes of the cirrhopod, and the feathers of a bird, and the fallacious deductions derived therefrom. The statements of Maier (p 112), Gerard (p. 106), Sir Robert Moray (p. 110), &c., prove that this fanciful misconception sprang from erroneous observation. The love of the marvellous inherent in mankind, and especially prevalent in times of ignorance and superstition, favoured its reception and adoption, and I believe that it would have been as widely circulated, and have met with equal credence, if the names of the cirripede and of the goose that was supposed to be its offspring had been far more dissimilar than, at first, they really were.

Setting aside several ingenious and far-fetched derivations that have been proposed, I think we may safely regard the word "barnacle," as applied to the cirrhopod, as a corruption of *pernacula*, the diminutive of *perna*, a bivalve mollusk, so-called from the similarity in shape of its shell to that of a ham—*pernacula* being changed to *bernacula*. In some old Glossaries *perna* is actually spelt *berna*.

To arrive at the origin of the word "barnacle," or "bernicle," as applied to the goose, we must understand that this bird, *Anser leucopsis*, was formerly called the "brent," "brant," or "bran" goose, and was supposed to be identical with the species, *Anser torquatus*, which is now known by that name. The Scottish word for "goose" is "clake," or "clakis," * and I think that the suggestion made long ago to Gesner † (1558), by his correspondent, Joannes Caius, is correct, that the word "barnacle" comes from "branclakis," or "barnclake," "the dark-coloured goose."

Professor Max Müller is of the opinion that its Latin name may have been derived from *Hibernicæ*, *Hibernicula*, *Bernicula*, as it was against the Irish bishops that Geraldus wrote, but I must say that this does not commend itself to me; for the name *Bernicula* was not used in the early times to denote these birds. Giraldus himself described them as *Bernacæ*, but they were variously known, also, as *Barliates*, *Bernestas*, *Barnetas*, *Barbates*, etc.

I agree with Dr. John Hill,‡ that "the whole matter that gave origin to the story is that the 'shell-fish' (cirripedes), supposed to have this wonderful production usually adhere to old wood, and that they have a kind of fibres hanging out of them, which, in some degree, resemble feathers of

---

* See the quotation from Hector Boetius, p. 101.
† 'Historia Animalium,' lib. iii. p. 110.
‡ 'History of Animals,' p. 422. 1752.

some bird. From this slight origin arose the story that they contained real birds: what grew on trees people soon asserted to be the fruit of trees, and, from step to step, the story gained credit with the hearers," till, at length, Gerard had the audacity to say that he had witnessed the transformation.

The Barnacle Goose is only a winter visitor of Great Britain. It breeds in the far north, in Greenland, Iceland, Spitzbergen, and Nova Zembla, and probably, also, along the shores of the White Sea. There are generally some specimens of this prettily-marked goose in the gardens of the Zoological Society in the Regent's Park, London; and they thrive there, and become very tame. In the months of December and January these geese may often be seen hanging for sale in poulterers' shops; and he who has tasted one well cooked may be pardoned if the suspicion cross his mind that the "monks of old," and "the bare-footed friars," as well as the laity, may not have been unwilling to sustain the fiction in order that they might conserve the privilege of having on their tables during the long fast of Lent so agreeable and succulent a "vegetable" or "fish" as a Barnacle Goose.

THE END.

LONDON: PRINTED BY WILLIAM CLOWES AND SONS, LIMITED,
STAMFORD STREET AND CHARING CROSS.

www.ingramcontent.com/pod-product-compliance
Lightning Source LLC
Chambersburg PA
CBHW031337160426
43196CB00007B/708